BlindSided

Dear Grief Series ... Book 2

by
Chenee' Gilbert, Ed.D.

SOUL DEEP PUBLISHING., LLC
AUSTELL, GEORGIA 30168

All Rights Reserved
Copyright © 2017 by Chenee' Gilbert
All rights reserved. This book or any portion thereof may not be reproduced or transmitted in any form or by any means, electronic or mechanical, including photocopying, recording, or by any information storage and retrieval system without permission in writing from the publisher.

ISBN: 978-0-692-96173-5
Library of Congress Control Number: 2017915923

Printed in the United States of America

First Printing

For information or to order additional books, please write:
Soul Deep Publishing
P.O. Box 1373
Austell, Georgia 30168
U.S.A.
678-750-3631

Or visit our web site
www.souldeeppublishing.com

Table of Contents

One 1
Two 35
Three 71
Four 95
Five..125
Six 167
About the Author 199

One

Don't Judge a Book By Its Cover

The easy days of summer arrived, and LaTrell had imagined what they would be like. She wanted to spend her mornings sleeping in, relaxing, and hanging around the house. However, Luis had a different plan. He arranged for LaTrell and Daryl to attend YMCA day camp. This meant they had to get up early, like they did for school. Every morning, LaTrell tried her best to persuade Luis that the camp was boring, useless, and any other negative words she could come up with. But after a few weeks of going, LaTrell began to warm up and even started looking forward to attending. There was one reason for her change of heart: Peaches. LaTrell had never known a girl like Peaches, and she was intrigued by someone about her age who seemed years ahead.

Peaches wore bright-colored polish with nail art on her toes and her fingernails. Almost all of the boys at the camp had a crush on her, because she stood out the most. Each week, Peaches attracted all sorts of attention with her different-colored hairstyles and hair extensions. LaTrell later learned that Peaches ran track for her school. Peaches loved to show skin. As long as the temperatures were at seventy degrees or above, you could bet that Peaches was going to wear either a spaghetti-strap dress or a pair of shorts with a halter top.

As much as LaTrell was drawn to Peaches, she often heard the voice in her head make judgments: *Hmph! Where in the world are her parents? Surely no parent would let their teenage daughter wear grown-up hairstyles like this.*

Nonetheless, LaTrell thought Peaches was the coolest girl ever. Some of the girls just wanted to be her friend because they thought that would make the boys like them, too. Others just liked to sit and watch as she told animated stories about her weekend fun. LaTrell wondered if Paulina would ever have let her shave her hair on the sides at the age of fourteen like the pop star Rihanna. There was little doubt that Luis would approve. He liked for LaTrell and Daryl to look and dress a certain way. Luis believed that clothes for people under the age of eighteen should not show their stomach or belly button and that a person's hair should be fixed according to his or her age.

Each day, LaTrell hung around Peaches and her

circle of friends, close enough to be nosy without being noticeable. Then she went home and stared at herself in the mirror. She wanted to see what she could change about her appearance. Besides braids, LaTrell was allowed to wear her hair in only a few styles, such as putting all her hair into a ponytail with a front bang or wearing a ponytail on top with a little hair left out in the back. LaTrell wore all of her hair down only for church or other special occasions. Paulina had been a stickler for making sure that LaTrell's hairstyles didn't involve too much use of the curling iron.

After Paulina's funeral, LaTrell convinced Luis to let her get braids to start her sixth-grade year. Luis asked what seemed like one hundred questions before he made his decision. LaTrell showed him a picture of the braid style and told him the name of the braider and the cost.

After she had provided him with all that information, LaTrell said, "Getting my hair braided would be cheaper for you."

"How do you figure that?" Luis asked.

"Well, Mama always made sure that I got my hair done every two weeks. If I get my hair braided, you wouldn't have to worry about paying to get my hair done, because braids usually last for about six weeks," LaTrell said.

"You got a point there," Luis said.

Needless to say, LaTrell ended up wearing braids for the second half of the school year. Every six or eight weeks, she took the braids down, washed her hair, and got it rebraided. For LaTrell's seventh-grade year, she wanted to try something different. She just didn't know what exactly. Peaches made it look so easy with her versatile hairstyles of different-colored clip-in hair extensions. *How come she gets to wear her hair and clothes any way she wants?* LaTrell said to herself.

One Friday, LaTrell's age group was scheduled to go on a field trip to the Everglades. The camp leaders had placed them in groups of two to complete assigned tasks before the buses arrived. LaTrell was paired with Peaches. She was excited and nervous now, concerned that Peaches might judge her based on the way she looked and her lack of fashion style. Since it would be a very hot and muggy day, LaTrell had pulled her hair back into a French braid.

When the kids boarded the bus and shared a seat with their partners, LaTrell sat next to the window to avoid any eye contact with Peaches. As she looked out the window on the bus ride, she felt two taps on her shoulder. LaTrell turned around to see Peaches smiling at her.

"Hey! I'm Peaches. What's your name?" Peaches asked with a smile.

"I'm LaTrell," LaTrell said with a nervous smile.

"Who put that braid in your hair?" Peaches asked.

"I did," LaTrell replied.

"Do you think that you could do my hair like that right now?" Peaches asked.

"If you have a comb and a brush, I can," LaTrell said.

"Yep! I stay prepared," Peaches said, as she opened her backpack and pulled out an orange wide-tooth comb and a skinny brown brush.

She handed the items over to LaTrell and then turned her back. LaTrell began to gently comb through Peaches' hair. Next, she brushed the edges upward and toward the center of the head. At the top of Peaches' head, she divided the hair into three sections. LaTrell crossed the sections, added hair to the section on each of the sides, and repeated the steps. She wanted to make sure that the French braid looked nice, so she took her time. It felt like it took a long time, but it was complete in less than five minutes. LaTrell got to the end and wrapped it with a rubber band to secure the braid.

Peaches leaned over the seat to get her friend's attention.

"Hey, Nikki! How does my hair look?" Peaches asked.

Nikki leaned in to get a closer look. She touched it and saw how smooth and neat it was.

"It looks really good!" Nikki said.

"Thanks to my little partner right here," Peaches said, pointing to LaTrell.

Peaches' comment made LaTrell feel special, like she was part of the clique.

"Girrrrl, I might let you do my hair like that one of these days. You did good!" Nikki said, looking at LaTrell.

"Yeah, you really hooked me up!" Peaches said, as she looked in a handheld mirror.

"Thanks," LaTrell said, smiling from ear to ear.

The bus arrived at the Everglades tourist center. Once the kids got off, they waited for the tour guide to give them directions.

"What school do you go to? What grade are you in?" Peaches asked during the tour.

"I attend H. Norman Middle, and I will be in seventh grade when school starts back up. What about you?" LaTrell asked.

"I attend Garden City Middle. I'll be an eighth grader for the second time, because I didn't past that stupid test," Peaches said, with a slight attitude.

"Oh, I'm sure you'll pass it this time around,"

LaTrell said, trying to sound convincing.

Peaches just looked at her and shrugged her shoulders. The group stopped near the reptile village, and the tour guide explained the different types of reptiles. No one in the group was paying attention. There were several conversations going on at one time. Peaches smacked her lips and held up her right hand to block the sun.

"I can't wait until tonight," Peaches said.

"Me either, girl," Nikki said, giving Peaches a high five.

"What's happening tonight?" LaTrell asked.

"Every Friday we go to this club for teenagers called Pack-N-Jam," Peaches said.

"Ooooh, that sounds fun," LaTrell said, trying to seem cool. "How do you get there?" she asked.

"We go with my big cousin. She just turned seventeen," said Nikki.

Wow! They get to do whatever they want, LaTrell said to herself.

During the rest of the field trip, all LaTrell thought about was how much freedom Peaches and the other girls had. They could do and wear anything they wanted. Suddenly, LaTrell felt jealous. She wanted to be able to experience things like them, too.

Later that evening, Daryl and LaTrell were at the dinner table with Luis, eating burgers and french fries, when Luis received a phone call from his brother and left the table.

"How was your field trip today?" Daryl asked.

"I guess it was okay. Hot and sticky is how I would describe it." LaTrell said, chewing her food.

"Well, it's better than being in the building all day. We didn't go outside today because our camp leader said she was allergic to the sun," Daryl said with disgust.

LaTrell stopped chewing her burger to chuckle.

"Allergic to the sun? I've never heard of that," LaTrell said.

"Yeah, and guess what her nickname is?" Daryl said, extending his hand in front of his face.

"What?" LaTrell asked.

"Her nickname is Sunny. How could you be named after something you're allergic to?" Daryl's voice was escalating with excitement. Then he got up from the table, seeming even more disappointed.

LaTrell shook her head and laughed even harder. Even though Daryl could be annoying he sure knew how to make her laugh.

After eating, LaTrell went into her room and closed the door. She climbed on top of the dresser to get as close to the mirror as she could. LaTrell took out her French braid and combed through her hair. *My hair color is so boring. It needs some color*, she thought. She knew of a few girls at camp who put cherry Kool-Aid in their hair. LaTrell knew that Luis and Daryl were leaving the house Saturday morning, so she decided that would be a good time for her to try it out.

The next morning, as planned, Luis and Daryl left the house at ten o'clock for the barbershop. LaTrell went to the kitchen to mix two packs of cherry Kool-Aid with half a cup of water and let it sit in a bowl. Then she shampooed and conditioned her hair. Afterward, LaTrell washed the conditioner out and gently squeezed the excess water from her ends of her hair with a towel.

LaTrell picked up the bowl of Kool-Aid and slowly poured the mixture on her hair while she leaned over the sink. Once she had poured out all of the mixture, she massaged it in. Next, LaTrell put a plastic cap on her head and sat under a hair dryer, to help lock in some of the color. LaTrell lasted under the dryer for only eight minutes because the heat was causing the Kool-Aid to smell like burned cherries.

LaTrell was so excited, she could feel adrenaline rushing through her entire body. She was finally doing something about her appearance. For a split second, she didn't even care what Luis was going to say. She washed the mixture out and towel-dried her hair, then combed it. To her amazement, the color had taken pretty well. LaTrell's natural color was dark brown; the Kool-Aid mixture had turned her hair to a strawberry color. Some areas were lighter than others.

God, please don't let people tease me by calling me Strawberry Shortcake, LaTrell said to herself.

LaTrell proceeded to blow-dry her hair. She parted a bang and brushed the rest of her hair back into a ponytail. Next, she curled the bang and the ends of the ponytail with her curling iron and pin-curled it. Suddenly, she started to care how Luis would react. She hurried to find a head scarf to tie down her hair. At least that would prevent Luis from seeing it until the next morning.

While LaTrell put the last hair supplies away, she heard the alarm chime. Luis and Daryl were back from the barbershop.

"Ewwww . . . what's that smell?" Daryl said, with his shirt over his nose.

"Yeah, what is that?" Luis asked.

"Oh, Shajuan let me borrow some conditioner. When I sat under the dryer, it made a funny smell," LaTrell said.

"Ain't nothing funny about that," Daryl said, waving his hands in front of his nose. "That is just stank!"

Luis asked, "What in the world is in that conditioner?"

"Um, I think it's a cherry flavor," LaTrell said.

"Well it smells more like rotten fruit," Luis said, as he opened the windows in the kitchen.

"The camp can use that conditioner scent to keep us from being bitten by mosquitoes. You don't have to worry about anyone getting close to you," Daryl said, shaking his head.

"Be quiet!" LaTrell snapped.

Later that evening, the smell finally faded away. Just as LaTrell was about to wash dishes, the phone rang.

LaTrell answered, "Hey, Shajuan!"

"How did you know it was me?" Shajuan asked, sounding puzzled.

"My dad just bought a new phone the other day, and the caller ID feature actually works," LaTrell said.

"Oh, wow! You mean Mr. Wiggins finally spent money on a new phone?" Shajuan joked.

"Guess what? I tried the cherry Kool-Aid color in my hair today," LaTrell said.

"You did? What does it look like? What did

your dad say?" Shajuan asked.

"He doesn't know yet. I told him I borrowed some cherry-flavored conditioner from you," LaTrell said.

"Oh, no you didn't!" Shajuan said.

"Yes I did," LaTrell said, "I colored my hair when he and Daryl went to get haircuts. I have a scarf on my hair now so he won't see the color until tomorrow morning."

LaTrell was waiting for Shajuan to say something. Instead, all she heard was silence.

"Hello?" LaTrell said.

"Girl, your daddy is going to be so mad," Shajuan said, with horror in her voice.

"No he's not! The most he can do is ground me and tell me to wash this stuff out of my hair," LaTrell said.

"Dang, we've only been out of school for three weeks. Summer just started—where did this bold side of you come from? Next, you'll be telling me you snuck out of the house to go somewhere," Shajuan said.

She was about to ramble on, when LaTrell blurted out the word *experimenting*.

"Hunh?" Shajuan asked.

"Seeing the girls at camp this summer made me want to try different things with my look. So I experimented with my hair first," LaTrell said, trying to sound confident.

"Hmm . . . I get it. But will your dad?" Shajuan asked.

"I sure hope he does. I'll keep you posted," LaTrell said.

"Yes, for sure. And I'll keep my fingers crossed," Shajuan said.

"Okay, bye!" LaTrell said.

After she hung up, LaTrell began to feel very nervous. She went to her room to write in her journal.

June 15

Hey, Mama! I think I may have messed up. I wanted to do something different with my hair, so I colored it with cherry Kool-Aid. I can hear you now: "Oh, LaTrell, what were you thinking?" Yeah, I know! I just wanted to have a moment to myself. I didn't even tell Shajuan about this. I'm afraid of how Dad will react in the morning when he sees my hair color for the first time. I'm sure I will be writing you sooner rather than later with some updates.

A bad thunderstorm rolled in on Sunday, so the Wiggins's ended up not going to church. *Whew! I get another day to keep my scarf on*, LaTrell said to herself.

On Monday morning, LaTrell woke up extra early. She wanted to make sure to get into the bathroom before anyone else. After she finished up, she opened the door and peeked out. Luis's and Daryl's bedroom doors were still closed. She tiptoed back to her room, put her clothes on, and decided to leave her head scarf on until she walked out of the house. She figured it would be too late for Luis to do anything.

LaTrell was already in the kitchen, eating cereal, when Luis came in. He had a puzzled look on his face.

"Well, good morning! I can't remember the last time you got up before me," Luis said, looking at LaTrell.

"I know, Dad. I think I went to bed too early," LaTrell said, as she continued to eat her cereal and glanced through a hair magazine.

Luis prepared his oatmeal. As he waited for his water to boil, he turned to face LaTrell and placed one elbow on the counter. LaTrell hoped Luis wasn't paying close attention to her hair. Even though it was covered, she still wasn't sure.

"What are you looking at, Dad?" LaTrell asked.

Luis shook his head as if he was coming out of a trance.

"Huh? Oh, um, I was thinking about everything that I have to do today. I guess I was daydreaming," Luis said.

Poor Dad, LaTrell thought. He tried to stick to Paulina's routine as much as possible. But ever since Paulina had passed, Luis's responsibilities had increased, so LaTrell and Daryl made sure they helped out around the house.

By the time Luis finished his oatmeal, Daryl ran into the kitchen as if he had seen a ghost.

"What spooked you?" LaTrell asked.

"Nothing. I overslept. I want to eat breakfast before we leave," Daryl said quickly.

"Well, you better hurry up! We're leaving in five minutes," Luis said.

Daryl moved faster. LaTrell's stomach begin to turn. The time for her to take off the scarf was getting closer. She went to her room and closed the door. Then she stood in front of the mirror and slowly untied the scarf, with her head lowered slightly. LaTrell's heartbeats sounded as loud as soldiers marching in an army. As soon as she felt the scarf fall on her shoulders, her eyes zoomed in on the mirror. To LaTrell's surprise, she couldn't really see the color. She opened the blinds to let more light in and leaned closer into the mirror.

I guess most of the color dissolved into the scarf, LaTrell thought.

Luis yelled, "Let's go!"

LaTrell grabbed her purse and headed for the front door. Once she stepped out onto the porch, her worst nightmare became a reality. As the sunlight hit the right side of her face, the sunrays picked up the cherry color in her hair. Daryl gave her a disgusted look and said, "Oh my God! You have dried-up blood in your hair. You must have been scratching your scalp while you were sleeping."

"It's not dried blood, you genius! I colored my hair with cherry Kool-Aid," LaTrell said matter-of-factly.

"Cherry Kool-Aid!" Luis and Daryl said in unison.

"Yes, most of the girls at camp have done it, so I wanted to give it a try," LaTrell said.

Luis looked at LaTrell and shook his head. "I don't know what to say. What were you thinking?" he asked.

"Well, I wanted to do something different with my hair. I don't think it looks bad," LaTrell said, trying to sound convincing.

"You better be glad we don't have time. But you can count on washing that stuff out of your hair as soon as you get home this evening," Luis said in a scolding voice.

"Yes, sir," LaTrell said, keeping her head lowered while she walked toward the car.

The ride to camp seemed longer than normal. The radio wasn't on, and Daryl didn't run his mouth. LaTrell looked out the window the entire time. Even though she had kind of expected Luis to get upset, her feelings were still hurt. *How come I couldn't do what I wanted with my hair?* she thought. She was glad Luis still allowed her to attend camp, though. He could have made her stay home, and LaTrell wanted to show off her new hair color. She hoped the other girls liked it. Finally, they reached the carpool line for drop-off.

"I'll see you all this evening," Luis said.

"All right, see you later, Dad," Daryl yelled, as he hopped out of the car.

LaTrell managed to mouth the word *bye* without making a sound. She closed the door and walked quickly to the entrance. As she entered the building, there were kids everywhere. Some stood in groups, laughing and joking. Others ran around. Since the lighting inside the building was a little dim, no one had noticed LaTrell's hair color yet.

LaTrell continued to walk through the building, toward the courtyard. In a small outside area with picnic tables, LaTrell's age group assembled before the camp mentors picked them up. The closer it got to eight o'clock, the more brightly the sunrays reflected off the windows and illuminated the courtyard.

There were three people from LaTrell's camp group already sitting at a table. Two girl cousins who also admired Peaches looked through a magazine together. The other was a cool basketball guy with headphones, listening to music. As LaTrell approached an empty picnic table, she slowed down her walking to soft footsteps. She hoped none of them noticed her as she took her seat. LaTrell sat down in slow motion. To her amazement, no one looked up or stopped what they were doing. She let out an internal sigh of relief.

She was about to take out a compact mirror to examine her hair before more kids showed up. Then, out of nowhere, she heard someone say loudly, "Who is *that*?"

LaTrell looked up and locked eyes with Peaches. The three students who hadn't noticed LaTrell before all noticed her now.

"OMG! My lil' partner, is that you?" Peaches

asked, as she walked closer.

At that moment, LaTrell felt like she was onstage under a bright spotlight. All eyes were on her.

LaTrell shook her head up and down to answer Peaches. "How does it look?" LaTrell asked.

Peaches took a step back, then circled around LaTrell.

"That color is poppin'! I'm just surprised to see you wearing a color that's so bold," Peaches said.

"I like it. It goes with your complexion," said one of the girls reading the magazine.

"Yeah, that color in your hair is dope, LaTrell," said the boy with the headphones.

LaTrell turned her head slightly to give them a half smile. LaTrell was surprised he knew her name.

"All right, Tasmanian Devils, let's head to our room," said Miss Jay, their camp counselor.

As LaTrell gathered her things, the counselor said, "Hey, LaTrell, I like that hair color. It looks cool on you."

"Thank you, Miss Jay!" LaTrell said.

As she walked toward the room, some of the kids and adults stared at her. LaTrell hoped that her hair wouldn't be the center of attention for long.

While working on an art project, Peaches walked over to LaTrell's table. "I've been looking at your hair all morning. Can I touch it?" Peaches asked.

"Yes, you can," LaTrell said.

Peaches gently touched the ends of LaTrell's hair.

"What did your mom say about your hair color?" Peaches asked.

"Huh? Oh . . . um . . . my mom died last year," LaTrell said, with a hesitant look.

"For real? Oh, I'm sorry—I didn't know," Peaches said.

"That's okay," LaTrell said. Then she added, "My dad saw my hair color for the first time this morning, and he was not happy. I think if he was a dragon, fire would have come out of his mouth."

Peaches chuckled. "Don't feel so bad. I remember coloring my hair with red Kool-Aid in the fifth grade," she said.

LaTrell gave Peaches the side-eye. *Oh, she must really think I'm a baby. The fifth grade? This girl really does whatever she wants*, LaTrell said to herself.

"Did you get in trouble?" LaTrell asked.

"Who, me? Ha—not really. See, even though I live with my mama and grandma, I don't really have any rules to follow. My grandma makes me do chores around the house and sometimes tries to boss me around, but it doesn't work. My mama is kind of like my big sister. She had me when she was fourteen. Most of the outfits I wear are hers. We share clothes. Some of the hairstyles and hair color I wear are styled by her," Peaches said with pride.

"Wow, you're lucky!" LaTrell said with amazement.

Peaches smiled. "Yeah, it's cool . . . I guess. Sometimes I wonder what it would be like if my mom put rules in place or disciplined me for some of the bad choices I make," she said, giving LaTrell a pensive look.

"Wait a minute. You've never been grounded, where you can't go outside or talk on the phone with your friends?" LaTrell asked.

"Um, no! Never," Peaches said, shaking her head. "Honestly, you're the only one I know who is being raised by her dad, let alone lived with two parents." She continued, "I think if my dad lived in my house, I wouldn't be able to do a lot of things that I do now, like going to the teen club, staying out till midnight on the weekends, and wearing certain clothes."

"Does your dad live in Florida?" LaTrell asked.

"No. After I was born, he and his mother moved

to Atlanta, Georgia. After finishing high school, he stayed there to help his uncle run his automotive shop. He usually comes down to visit once or twice a year. When I was in fourth grade, he sent for me to attend his wedding. I haven't been back since. I don't think his wife understands me." Peaches sighed and shrugged her shoulders.

"We talk once a week, though. For some reason, he's always asking about the type of people I hang around with, my grades, my homework, and if I have a career choice in mind," Peaches said. She sounded aggravated.

"What's wrong with that?" LaTrell asked.

"I dunno. Shoot, ask me normal questions, like what's my favorite color," Peaches said.

LaTrell chuckled. "Peaches, you are funny. Those *are* normal questions he's asking you."

"Hmph, if you say so. My mama or grandma never asks me questions like that," Peaches said.

"I think your dad is just trying to find out what you're up to, to show that he cares about you," LaTrell said.

Peaches looked at LaTrell and rolled her eyes to the ceiling.

"I know talking to your dad feels weird. I felt the same way at first. After my mom died, I talked to my dad more. He listens to what I have to say, offers advice, or tries to help fix a problem. It's a good feeling when you can communicate with your parent without feeling scared or being fussed at. Give it a try with your dad," LaTrell said.

Peaches looked at LaTrell.

"Oh, before I forget, my dad told me I need to wash the color out as soon as I get home this evening. The problem is, I don't know how. Do you?" LaTrell asked.

"Girl, you are asking the right person, 'cause you know I am the queen of Kool-Aid hair," Peaches said, pointing her thumb toward her with a confident smirk. "I'm going to tell you straight up, it usually takes two to three hair washes before the color is completely gone. Okay, this is what you need. You need to write this down," Peaches said, motioning for LaTrell to get a pencil and a piece of paper.

"You will need a wide-tooth comb, shampoo, conditioner, a plastic cap, baking soda, and a small can of tomato juice," Peaches said.

"Canned tomato juice?" LaTrell asked, giving Peaches a puzzled look.

"Mm-hmm," Peaches said. "Now, when you wash your hair, you need to make sure to get the water as hot as possible. Shampoo and rinse your hair. Next, you take the baking soda and sprinkle it all over your hair. Massage it in, and let it sit for at least five minutes; then rinse it out. Then you will pour the bottle of tomato juice over your hair. You also need to work this through the ends of your hair for two to three minutes. Rinse the tomato juice out. Finally, put the conditioner on your hair. Comb your hair and put on a plastic cap for ten minutes. Rinse the conditioner out. Dry it and style it like you want," Peaches said, as if she was giving a presentation.

"That's a lot of steps," LaTrell said, looking at Peaches in shock.

"I know it seems like a lot, because this is your first time. But the more you do it, the more you get used to it," Peaches said.

"What do you mean, *the more you do it*? Do you mean the more I Kool-Aid-color my hair?" LaTrell asked.

"Oh yeah, I forgot," Peaches said, laughing. "This is your first *and* last time."

Later that evening, LaTrell prepared to wash her hair. Luckily, all of the materials were already in the house. LaTrell followed Peaches' directions step by step. After she had completed the last step, she towel-dried her hair. LaTrell leaned closer toward the mirror to see the results.

"Hmm . . . not bad," she said to herself. Letting

the baking soda sit in her hair for twenty minutes had worked in her favor. It had picked up almost all of the red particles from the Kool-Aid.

LaTrell blow-dried her hair and then pulled it back into a ponytail. When she opened the bathroom door, Luis came around the corner. He stopped in his tracks when he saw LaTrell.

"Did the process work?" Luis asked.

"Yes, the baking soda lifted a lot of the Kool-Aid color. There's still a little bit left in the middle, though," LaTrell said, patting the middle of her head.

Luis turned on the hall light and walked closer to LaTrell to get a better look.

"Yep, it looks like the baking soda did the trick," Luis said.

"LaTrell, I know you didn't like my reaction to your hair color. I need you to understand that as a parent I am responsible for making sure you are properly taken care of. This means providing food, shelter, clothes, and supervision. That red hair color was not appropriate for your age. I see that you like to take chances, and something tells me that this won't be your last time trying something new. From this point, ask or tell me what you would like to wear or do with your hair. I'll try my best to meet you halfway. Trust me, you don't want to look grown before your time. Enjoy your youth and natural beauty while you can. Understand?" Luis said.

"Yeah, I do. It's just that a lot of the girls at camp wore different hair colors and I thought it looked cool. The girls are only a few years older than me. Why are they allowed to wear hair color?" LaTrell asked.

"I can't speak for their parents. Everyone is different," Luis said, shaking his head in slow motion. "You and Daryl are my only concern."

LaTrell let out a sigh and said, "Okay, Dad!"

Luis continued to walk toward his bedroom, and LaTrell walked toward hers. She sat up against the headboard and reached for her journal.

June 17
Here One Minute, Gone the Next
Hey, Mama. I guess you see my title. That's exactly what happened to my hair color. I must admit that even though I was digging the color, it was a little too grown for me. After getting in trouble with Daddy, I don't think I will pull another stunt like this. Would you have been as upset as Daddy? The best part is, I followed the directions that my friend

Peaches from camp gave me to get the color out. It worked! Remember, she's the popular one I told you about who wears the latest hairstyles and clothes? Mama, Peaches can stay out to midnight on the weekends. And she is only in the eighth grade! Can you believe that? I haven't told Dad about her yet. I already know that he wouldn't approve of me hanging around her. I can also picture you saying, "Be careful around that girl Peaches, LaTrell. She acts a little too fast." LOL. That may be true. But she's a nice person. I'm trying to get her to communicate with her dad like I do with mine. I hope she gives it a try. I'll keep you posted. Love you, Mama!

The next day, LaTrell woke up with a big yawn and stretched her arms. She got up and checked herself out in the bathroom mirror. She took the scarf off. Her hair looked like it had returned to its natural color. As LaTrell left the bathroom, Daryl came out of his bedroom. He caught sight of

LaTrell's hair and stopped walking. Daryl clapped three times and said, "Bravo, bravo. Now, *this* is more like it. You look normal again, not like you belong in a horror movie."

LaTrell rolled her eyes at Daryl and brushed past him to go back to her room. *Ugh, he gets on my nerves*, she said to herself.

LaTrell put her clothes on and brushed her hair up into a high ponytail.

"Okay, guys, I don't hear anyone eating breakfast. Let's get a move on," Luis yelled.

LaTrell heard footsteps running toward the kitchen, and she knew it was Daryl. As he sat down and began stuffing his mouth with cereal, LaTrell fixed herself a slice of toast with butter and jelly.

"That's all you're eating?" Daryl asked.

"Mm-hmm," LaTrell said.

"It's time to get in the car," Luis said.

LaTrell put her toast in a sandwich bag to eat in the car. Daryl put the cereal bowl up to his lips to drink the remaining milk. When he finished, his mouth was covered with milk. "Man, that was good!" Daryl said, wiping his lips. Luis and LaTrell looked at Daryl and then at each other and shook their heads.

During the car ride to camp, LaTrell thought about the talk she'd had with Peaches. She felt sorry for her. It seemed like Peaches was raising herself.

When LaTrell and Daryl arrived at camp, LaTrell's group was already in the room. As she walked in, Ms. Jay was sorting papers.

"LaTrell, you switched up on me again?" Ms. Jay asked, smiling.

"Yes, ma'am. No more hair color for me right now," LaTrell said, as she smiled back.

LaTrell took her seat and glanced around the room. Nikki waved from across the room. LaTrell waved back. Then she caught Peaches' attention. LaTrell pointed to her hair and mouthed, "It worked!"

Peaches smiled and flashed two thumbs up.

The last few weeks of June passed quickly. The Fourth of July appeared as quickly as the sunrise. Luis didn't have any out-of-town trips planned. Instead, Grandma Adela and Aunt Roberta came down to visit with a few of Daryl and LaTrell's cousins. They spent the three-day weekend at the water park, movies, and Dave & Buster's. Before the family left on Sunday, they went to put fresh flowers on Paulina's grave. LaTrell saw the sadness in everyone's eyes. After a few minutes, everyone walked back to the cars and said their goodbyes.

After the holiday weekend, it was back to

attending camp as usual. LaTrell sat in the courtyard area and worked on a word-search puzzle. She looked up to see Peaches moving LaTrell's purse to the side to sit down.

"What's up, my lil' partner?" Peaches said with a smile.

"Hey, Peaches!" LaTrell said, as she put down her pencil.

"My dad came down this weekend from Georgia. This time, we got a chance to really hang out and do things, like go bowling and eat out at a restaurant," Peaches said. "And then guess what? He took me shopping, and I let him choose a few of my outfits for the new school year," Peaches said, her eyes wide.

"What?" LaTrell said, feeling her jaw drop.

"I know, right? Honestly, the outfits that he chose for me are cute. I think he kind of gets my style. He showed me that I can still dress cool and hip without having to show a lot of skin. He also taught me how to eat and order at a restaurant. I had no idea that both of my elbows didn't belong on the table. I don't really eat at those types of restaurants," Peaches said.

"Yeah, my mom used to tell me the same thing," LaTrell said, smiling.

"I had a good time. All of the attention was on

me. He wasn't on his cell phone, talking with his friends or anything. He told me to ask him anything, and I did. I learned a lot of information that I was never told. And because of our talks, I feel more comfortable talking with him now. He said he's going to get me a cell phone for my birthday so that I can call him anytime I want," Peaches said, giving LaTrell the brightest smile.

"Wow, Peaches. I'm so happy for you. You're even talking different," LaTrell said.

Peaches chuckled and tapped LaTrell's arm, saying, "Girl, you're so silly!"

When LaTrell got home, she couldn't wait to update Paulina on Peaches and her dad.

July 7

Hey, Mama. Good news, good news. You know my friend Peaches from camp? She finally started communicating with her dad. You should see her, Mama. Her attitude has even changed. I'm so happy for her. Oh yeah, did you like the beautiful flowers that Grandma Adela and Aunt Roberta left on your grave? I know you're smiling. As long as you keep doing so, I'm okay. Talk to you later, Mama! Love you.

LaTrell placed the journal on her nightstand. Then she lay on her back, staring at her pink walls. Her talk with Peaches reminded her of the assembly she had attended last May, at the end of the school year. One of the topics discussed was empathy and compassion. The speaker stated that middle-school years are critical. Preteens should be encouraged to express and discuss their feelings without being made to feel wrong. Not being judged had helped Peaches open up to her father. *And it surely has helped me*, LaTrell thought.

Chapter 1 Questions

1. Can you think of a time when you were being judged?

2. Can you think of a time when you judged someone wrongly?

3. Have you ever crossed the line by not being true to yourself because you were afraid of being judged (e.g., taking a puff of a cigarette, stealing, or visiting a place without permission)?

Two

Speak Up or Else!

After the Fourth of July passed, the number of the camp participants decreased a great deal, even for field trips. Class size dropped from fifteen to twenty students to only seven or eight. Some kids went to visit their grandparents for a week or two. Others just stopped coming altogether, including Peaches. Now that summer camp wasn't fun anymore, LaTrell and Daryl made a daily habit of complaining to Luis about how much they dreaded going. To their surprise, Luis finally gave in and let them stay home the last few weeks before school started.

On one of her first days home, LaTrell sat on her bed cross-legged while she looked through a magazine. Aunt Kat had given LaTrell a one-year subscription to *Seventeen* for her birthday, and LaTrell wanted to get some fashion ideas before she went back-to-school shopping that weekend.

The morning of their shopping trip, Luis said, "All right, guys, we're not spending more than two hours here. Do you know what stores you'd like to shop in?"

"Yep," LaTrell and Daryl answered at the same time. Then Daryl added, "Hey, Dad, what's our budget?"

"What's *our* budget? Oh, do you plan to help me pay for your clothes?" asked Luis, with a smile both kids recognized.

"Ha ha, Dad, you're funny. No, I wanted to see if there's room in the budget for me to get a Miami Heat limited-edition hoodie," Daryl said.

"A Miami Heat hoodie? Where did you see one of those?" Luis asked.

"My favorite rapper wore one on the music awards show that LaTrell and I watched last month. Besides the Miami Heat being my favorite basketball team, this hoodie looks real cool and helps you pull all the ladies," Daryl said, while posing like a model.

"Eww," LaTrell said, curling her lip.

"Lil' man, Florida doesn't produce enough cold days or winters for a jacket like that. Your focus should be on choosing five shirts, two pairs of shorts, three pairs of pants, and two pairs of shoes," Luis said, smirking at Daryl.

"Oh, Dad," Daryl said, raising both hands in the air.

"Come on. Let's get a move on. I want to get to the mall as soon as it opens, to beat the crowds,"

Luis said. *And get out of there as fast as I can*, he added silently to himself.

As planned, the Wigginses parked just as the mall opened. Since Daryl liked to wear Ralph Lauren clothes, they went first to Macy's, which was having a sale. Daryl walked in front to lead Luis to his section. LaTrell lagged behind to study the mannequins dressed in stylish clothes for girls. Inspired by some of the outfits Peaches had worn to summer camp, she wanted a different look for the upcoming school year.

Hmm, I'm really digging these fashionable leggings, LaTrell said to herself, holding up a pink-and-black zebra-print pair.

"Found it!" Daryl yelled, his voice echoing through the whole department.

LaTrell wandered over to where Luis and Daryl were.

"Ahem," Luis said, clearing his throat. "You're looking in the wrong place, son. You need to be over here with me," Luis said, pointing to Daryl's section.

"Oh," Daryl said, looking at Luis, then at the items he held in his hand, then back at Luis.

Daryl hung the shirts in his hand back on the rack and walked over to Luis. He removed shirts from Luis's arm one at a time and carefully analyzed each one. Daryl spent at least twenty minutes walking around before he made a decision. He finally picked six shirts, three pairs of shorts, and two pairs of jeans.

Luis and Daryl went to the cashier to check out.

"Dad, what about the hoodie?" Daryl asked.

"Uh, we'll come back during Labor Day weekend to purchase jackets. We still have time before those cool fall mornings creep in," Luis said, as he paid for Daryl's clothes.

Then Luis said, "Okay, LaTrell, it's your turn. Where to next?"

"Oh boy! Here we go with Ms. Fashion Queen," Daryl said, shaking his head.

"Will you hush? Did you hear me complain when you walked in circles, trying to make your decision?" LaTrell asked.

"That's right. She sure didn't. Now, let her have her time," Luis said.

Daryl looked at LaTrell and Luis and gave a little shrug.

"I want to go back over to the teen section. I saw some cool leggings that I like," LaTrell said.

Once they got to the juniors' department, LaTrell gathered the items that she wanted to try on. Daryl and Luis sat in the waiting area.

LaTrell appeared from behind the curtain,

modeling a pair of leggings with an asymmetrical top that stopped at the waist in the front and hung long in the back.

"What do you think, Dad?" LaTrell asked.

"I think it looks nice on you. Do you like it?" Luis asked.

"Yep!" LaTrell said, turning from side to side in front of the mirror.

Just as LaTrell was about to turn around to go behind the curtain, Daryl pointed at LaTrell's legs and asked, "Why do your legs look like drumsticks?"

"It's in her genes," Luis said. "She is definitely shaped like her mother." He and LaTrell looked at each other and smiled.

LaTrell tried on clothes for another half an hour, before she finally appeared with an armful of items. Daryl was curled up in his seat, playing with a Nintendo 3DS that he had brought with him. "About time!" he said, looking up from his game.

Luis was sitting in his chair, cracking his knuckles and whistling a tune. "All ready to go?" he asked.

"I think so," LaTrell said.

Luis helped LaTrell carry some of the clothes to the checkout counter.

"Um, Dad, I thought you said LaTrell and I were on a budget." Daryl said.

"That's right," Luis said.

"Well, it sure looks like LaTrell went over hers. We haven't even bought shoes yet," Daryl said.

"Leave your sister alone. She should be okay," Luis said.

"Good afternoon," the cashier said in a cheerful voice.

"Good afternoon," the Wiggins clan replied.

"Ooh, I see someone has an eye for fashion," the cashier said, smiling at LaTrell. She rang up each piece with excitement. When the cashier hit the TOTAL button, she said, "Woohoo, somebody caught a good sale today!"

Luis and LaTrell turned the monitor around to look at the amount.

"All right, that's what I'm talking about—good-quality clothes at low prices," Luis said, as he handed the clerk his debit card.

Daryl didn't seem fazed at all by the excitement. He was ready to go pick out sneakers.

"How about that? I think this is the first time you two have shopped in the same store. We usually visit at least three or four stores for you, LaTrell," Luis said.

"Yeah, at *least*!" Daryl said.

"I know. I figured since Grandma Adela and Aunt Roberta may come down for Labor Day, I'll wait to go shopping with them at the other stores I like," LaTrell said, smiling.

"Look at you, spending someone else's money without them knowing it," Luis said with a chuckle.

LaTrell and Daryl laughed, too.

"Whew! Boy, what a morning. Both of you are squared away for school. We will attend the back-to-school drive held at the church next weekend. The book bags and school supplies you receive should be enough for the first few months of school. What do you think?" Luis asked.

"Yeah, they will," LaTrell and Daryl said in agreement.

Once they got home, LaTrell and Daryl rushed to their rooms with their bags. First, LaTrell laid her outfits on her bed. Next, she hung them on a hanger. Then she sorted the outfits into two categories: "clothes to wear the first week of school" and "no hurry." Finally, she arranged them in the order in which she would wear them the first week of school.

Daryl threw his bag of clothes on his bed. He was more concerned with his new pair of sneakers than with anything else. He opened the shoebox and took out one of the sleek navy blue–and-white shoes to inspect it more closely. *I will definitely make sure no one steps on these*, he said to himself.

LaTrell was still standing at her closet, her left hand cupping her chin and her right arm folded underneath. Finally, she let out a sigh, walked to her bed, sat up against the headboard, and reached for her journal.

August 7

Hi Mama! We went school shopping today. I think Dad is starting to get the hang of it. Even though he still sets a time limit for what we do and the places we go, if it takes longer than usual, he just goes with the flow. Ha ha . . . I'm picturing the surprised look on your face. Yes, I know, right? Who would ever have thought Luis Wiggins would go mall shopping without rushing? :) Oh yeah—Dad doesn't play when it comes to that spending budget, either. Using the puppy eyes doesn't work on him. I know that made you smile. We still miss you being here with us Mama. :)

The first day of school arrived. LaTrell was excited, as usual. She woke up fifteen minutes before her alarm clock went off. Since she had decided not to wear braids yet, she took extra time to neatly brush her hair up in a high ponytail and then formed a bun. After the bun was secured, LaTrell took a step back from the mirror and turned her head from side to side. She walked over to the closet to take her clothes off the hanger. As soon as she slid into her shirt and leggings, the alarm clock went off and she heard a knock on her bedroom door.

"I'm already up, Dad," LaTrell said through the door, while turning the buzzer off.

Luis opened the door just enough to peek inside LaTrell's room.

"Oh, and you're dressed, too?" he asked with surprise.

"Yes, I got up earlier to get my hair together. And I'm also a little excited," LaTrell said.

"Yeah, you and your brother have both always been excited on the first day of school. Okay, I'll let you finish getting yourself together. There are waffles and bacon in the microwave. You better get in there before your brother does," Luis said, smiling.

"Mmm, waffles. You don't have to tell me

twice. I'll be out in two minutes," LaTrell said, gathering her things.

As LaTrell put on her shoes, she glanced at the journal sitting on her nightstand and decided to write some more before she left.

August 9

Good morning, Mama! Today is the first day of school. Can you believe I'm already in my second year of middle school? Me either. I can't wait to tell you about my day. Right now I need to hurry up and get to the kitchen before Daryl eats up all of the waffles. Love you. :)

By the time LaTrell arrived in the kitchen, Daryl was on his third waffle. She looked at Daryl and shook her head with disgust as she began to fix her plate.

"Are you guys finished? We need to leave the house soon," Luis called out.

"Yep!" LaTrell and Daryl yelled.

LaTrell and Daryl stuffed the last bites into their mouths and quickly got up to throw away their plates. Before walking out of the front door, LaTrell checked herself out in the living room wall mirror.

Daryl walked up close behind her and said, "Yeah, you still look the same as you did five minutes ago."

"Ugh, *move*," LaTrell said, as she pushed him away.

"Stop giving your sister a hard time," Luis said to Daryl.

"I don't mean to, Dad, but it looks like I have to keep everyone on track around here," Daryl said with confidence.

LaTrell rolled her eyes, and Luis laughed and said, "Boy, you sure are funny."

As Luis drove, he turned down the radio to talk to LaTrell and Daryl.

"Hey, guys, I want to wish both of you a great first day. I know it gets a little tough every now and then without Mom here, but in spite of that, I think we're adjusting very well. Remember, above anything else, we're family first . . ."

"And we communicate second," LaTrell and Daryl said, finishing the sentence.

"That's right—no thoughts or feelings go unheard. Got it?" Luis asked.

"Got it!" LaTrell and Daryl echoed back.

Soon after their talk, Luis pulled up in front of Daryl's school.

"Bye, Big Head," LaTrell said.

"Takes one to know one," Daryl said, hurrying out of the car.

"Have a good day, son!" Luis said.

"I will, Dad. Thanks!" Daryl said, as he walked away toward the front door.

As Luis continued on toward LaTrell's school, LaTrell spotted Chandler walking to the bus stop.

"Dad, there's Chandler. Can we give him a ride?" LaTrell asked.

"Sure, why not? Get his attention," Luis said.

LaTrell rolled down her window to call Chandler's name and motioned for him to get in the car.

"Boy, I'm glad to see you all. I did not feel like running from those stray dogs that hang around the gray house at the bus stop," Chandler said, wiping sweat from his forehead.

LaTrell and Luis both chuckled.

When Luis pulled up in front of the school. LaTrell let out a sigh.

"All right, sweetie, have a great day. You too, Chandler!" Luis said, as LaTrell and Chandler exited the car.

"Thanks, Dad," LaTrell said.

"Thanks again for the ride, Mr. Luis," Chandler said.

"Anytime," Luis said. He sat and watched them go for a few more seconds, then drove off.

While walking up the sidewalk, Chandler immediately started running his mouth about what teachers and lunch period he hoped to have. He was about to start another sentence, when suddenly he paused.

"LaTrell, I can't put my finger on it, but something is different about you," he said, raising his left eyebrow.

"Different how?" LaTrell asked.

"I'm not sure. Maybe it's the hairstyle," Chandler said, while taking another long look at LaTrell.

"Maybe," LaTrell said, shrugging her shoulders. Then she glanced over at Chandler and noticed that he was wearing the latest name-brand jeans, shirt, and shoes.

"Chandler, you are dressed sharp today," LaTrell said, tugging on his shirtsleeve.

"Don't trip, LaTrell—you know I'm always fly," Chandler said, with his chest poked out and a slight dip in his walk. Then he added, with a big smile, "My dad is stationed in Germany now. Since the clothes are a little cheaper there, he sent at least four big boxes of clothes and shoes. Man, it was like Christmas in July."

LaTrell laughed. "I bet it was," she said.

When they approached the steps to the school, LaTrell immediately flashed back to the first day of sixth grade. She remembered being excited and nervous. This year, she walked up the steps with ease and confidence.

"Girls first," Chandler said, while opening the door for her.

"I see we learned some manners over the summer," LaTrell said with a smirk.

"Nope! I've always had manners. I just choose when I want to use them," Chandler said matter-of-factly.

As LaTrell and Chandler entered the building, they were greeted by the principal, Mr. Willingham, and other faculty members. There were signs directing students from each grade level to different places. Seventh-graders reported to the library to pick up their schedules. LaTrell and Chandler went down one flight of stairs and proceeded down the hall. On the way there, they passed Ms. Nichols, standing by her classroom door.

"Hi, Ms. Nichols!" LaTrell said with a smile.

"Well, hello there, LaTrell! Welcome back. Did

you have a nice summer?" Ms. Nichols asked.

"Yes, ma'am," LaTrell replied.

"That is awesome. Well, if I don't see you anymore, have a great first week of school. Don't be a stranger, now," Ms. Nichols said, waving her hand.

"I won't," LaTrell said, returning the wave. Then she caught up with Chandler, who had walked ahead to chat with some friends.

Inside the library were five tables and big white posters with letters of the alphabet written on them. Students got in line according to the first letter of their last name.

"Well, I guess I'm the alpha and you're the omega," Chandler said, patting LaTrell on the shoulder.

"Really, Chandler?" she said sarcastically.

Since Chandler's last name was Adams, he stood in line at the first table, while LaTrell went to the last table because her last name began with the letter *W*.

LaTrell received her schedule and noticed that Technology was listed as the first course. When she read to the end, her eyes grew big. *Band! I have band this semester?* she said to herself.

Since Paulina had died, LaTrell and Daryl hadn't played the piano, which, along with the flute, had been Paulina's favorite instrument to play. On certain days of the week, Paulina had given piano lessons. LaTrell and Daryl had not been excused and had been required to practice, just like the rest of the students.

LaTrell took her time walking down the hall. All sorts of emotions and questions started to fill her head.

"What if I've forgotten everything you taught me, Mama?" LaTrell said in a whisper.

But within an instant, she heard her mom's voice saying, *It's okay. I'm watching.*

LaTrell immediately felt comforted, and she felt the worried look on her face turning into a peaceful one. *You're always on time, Mama*, she said to herself, as she continued walking to class.

August 9

Woosah! One day down, Mama; 179 more to go. My classes seem like they're going to be okay. Mr. Barnett, who plays in the band at church, is our teacher. Isn't that cool? We won't touch instruments until after Labor Day. Mr. Barnett says we need to learn basic information first, like music note counts and music terms. Which instrument do you think I should choose? Keyboard? Flute? I hope you help me decide sooner rather than later. Thanks again for calming my nerves earlier today. There's this feeling I get when I hear your voice. I can't describe it in words. I am thankful to know that my own mother is my guardian angel and has my back. I miss you, Mama. Mwah!

It was a dreary September Sunday, and Luis turned on his right side. His half smile turned into a serious look. He ran his hand across the pillows Paulina had once slept on.

"Gone too soon," Luis said, shaking his head slowly.

Nothing could have prepared me for this. I hope you are pleased with how I'm raising the kids. We need to get back on track with going to church on a more regular basis. The times we have attended, I still expect to see you in the choir stand. I'm getting a little better, though, Luis thought to himself, and smiled.

"I guess we will try to go to church next

Sunday," Luis said aloud, as he made himself comfortable to lie back down in the bed.

Then a soft voice whispered, "Why not today?"

Luis quickly sat up and looked to his left and his right to make sure he wasn't hearing things. He chuckled and said, "Hmph, I should have known you were listening to my thoughts."

With that, Luis eased out of bed and woke up LaTrell and Daryl for church.

After they ate breakfast, they all got dressed. LaTrell put on a nice, long-sleeved white shirt with a black skirt and black patent-leather flats. Luis emerged from his room wearing a smoke-gray suit. LaTrell always thought Luis looked handsome and very important in suits. Daryl seemed to be full of himself lately. He wore a T-shirt that read IF NOT ME, WHO ELSE? along with a pair of denim jeans without a belt, which caused the top of his boxers to show, and his new pair of sneakers.

"What in the world?" Luis asked, looking confused. "Where do you think you're going?"

"To church with you," Daryl said.

"I don't think so. You need to return to your room to put on a dress shirt and a pair of slacks," Luis ordered.

"But it gets hot in church," Daryl said.

"I'll make sure the usher gives you a fan. Now, hurry up and go change. You know how fast the church fills up," Luis said.

"Yes, sir," Daryl said, turning around with his head hanging down.

LaTrell shook her head and thought, *My poor little brother thinks some of the high school–age boys in the neighborhood dress so cool that he wants to be like them.* LaTrell knew the feeling. She felt the same way about Peaches.

When the family entered the doors of the church, they were greeted by ladies standing on each side, dressed in all white. Each person was given a program, and fans were available upon request. Luis looked back to make sure Daryl got one. Another usher walked them to the fifth pew. After they were seated, they joined in with the deacons to sing the first hymn.

As LaTrell looked straight ahead, she felt eyes watching them. She looked over at Sister Johnson, who nodded and smiled. LaTrell waved and smiled back. Soon, the piano and the drums began to play. LaTrell's eyes automatically went to the piano player. She wanted to see who had replaced Paulina.

Paulina had been the pianist for the church for a long time. If she wasn't playing the piano, she would be directing one of the choirs. When she became ill, she had to stop participating, and the church hired a temporary pianist. Each time LaTrell came to church, it felt weird not seeing Paulina in the choir stand.

LaTrell was deep in thought, reminiscing about Paulina, when a sweet-sounding voice filled the church and snapped LaTrell out of her daze. It was Sister Osborne, who had a voice like Whitney Houston's. Anytime she led a song, it either moved people to tears or made them stand up and clap along. This Sunday, more than half of the church was standing up and clapping. The few people who remained seated were foot tapping, clapping, or waving their hands in the air. As the song was coming to an end, it sounded like a concert inside the church. There was so much noise.

Luis leaned over to LaTrell and Daryl and said, "That Sister Osborne knows she can sing."

"She sure can," LaTrell said.

LaTrell turned to Daryl, who was looking very uncomfortable.

"What's wrong?" LaTrell asked.

"Man, it's so hot in here, I'm sweating like I've been outside, playing football. This fan ain't working," Daryl said, while moving his wrist up and down in fast motion.

"Tell Dad you have to go to the bathroom," LaTrell said.

Daryl did exactly that. When he had been gone for more than fifteen minutes, Luis told LaTrell to go and check on Daryl. She stood up and walked out, holding her right index finger up. This was an old tradition of the Baptist Church and a quiet way of saying, "Excuse me" or, "Pardon me." LaTrell walked toward the bathroom and noticed Daryl sitting in the corner of the lobby. LaTrell startled him when she touched his shoulder.

"Why are you sitting over here?" LaTrell asked.

"Because," Daryl said, with an angry look on his face.

"Because what?" LaTrell asked.

"A few of the boys from the Junior Christian Gentleman group were hanging out in the bathroom. As I washed my hands, some of them started cracking jokes about me not being babied by Mama anymore. They also said that since Mama wasn't around anymore, I could make decisions for myself now. I told them to shut up and at least my dad was around to help me make decisions. Then one of the boys raised his fist to me and said, 'Where's your dad at now?' But someone came into the bathroom and scared them off." Daryl looked up at LaTrell as if he was insulted.

The Junior Christian Gentlemen were a group at the church for boys between the ages of eight and ten. The boys often met once a week to do activities to help them make the right choices, take responsibility, and stand together in unity.

"Don't pay any attention to them. They're just trying to be troublemakers. I know what they said was mean, but sometimes you need to ignore what people say," LaTrell said.

"Oh, come on! I wasn't going to let them talk about my mama like that. I had to speak up for myself to let them know I'm not a pushover," Daryl said.

LaTrell nodded her head to let Daryl know she understood how he felt. "Yeah, you're right. Have you calmed down some?" she asked.

"Yeah, I feel a little better now," Daryl said.

"Well, we better get back to our seats before Dad comes looking for us," LaTrell said.

"Okay," Daryl said.

When LaTrell turned around to walk, Daryl grabbed her wrist. "Promise you won't tell Dad about this," he said.

"Okay, I won't," LaTrell said, taking a deep breath.

LaTrell and Daryl got back to their seats just as the preacher began the sermon.

Luis looked at them and whispered, "I was just about to come and find you all. What took you so long?"

Since they were in church, LaTrell and Daryl really didn't want to lie. Daryl told him there were a lot of people trying to use the bathrooms.

Luis looked strangely at both of them, as if he knew there was something else not being said. But he shrugged his shoulders and tuned back to the sermon.

Before service ended, the welcome announcements were read.

"Attention, all members. It's time for our Fall Festival again. This year we would like for everyone to participate. There are sign-up sheets for different committees posted in the multipurpose room. The Fall Festival will be on September thirtieth. Please save the date. Thank you."

The Fall Festival was always a big extravaganza for the church. People got a chance to show off their talents, baking skills, and crafts.

"Are you going to participate this year?" Luis asked LaTrell and Daryl.

"I don't know," Daryl said.

"Me either," LaTrell said.

After church, Luis went over to speak to one of his childhood friends. LaTrell and Daryl went to the multipurpose area, where the sign-up sheets were.

Shad, the Junior Christian Gentlemen group leader, came over and gave LaTrell a hug and high-fived Daryl.

He looked at Daryl and said, "The group is going to perform a step show for the Fall Festival. We really would like for you to participate. So, how about it?"

Judging by the look on Daryl's face, LaTrell could tell he was still thinking about what had happened earlier with the other members of the group.

"I'll think about it," Daryl said.

"Well, don't wait too long. We begin practice this weekend. I look forward to seeing you," Shad said, as he shook Daryl's hand.

He saw another member and immediately walked away to catch up with them.

LaTrell heard someone call her name from behind.

"Hey, LaTrell, long time no see," said Carmen.

"I know, it's been a while," LaTrell said.

"Are you thinking about signing up for a committee?" Carmen asked.

"I don't know. I haven't decided what I'm going to do. What about you?" LaTrell asked.

"I'm going to sing that new song by Yolanda Adams," Carmen said confidently.

"Oh, that should be nice," LaTrell said, trying not to look too surprised. Carmen was a terrible singer. She and LaTrell had both grown up singing in the junior choir, which consisted of children ranging from three to ten years old.

"Since your mom passed, no one hardly sees you around the church anymore. When are you going to start back participating with the Junior Rubies? Don't you think your mom would want you to continue?" Carmen asked.

Carmen's comment caught LaTrell off guard, and LaTrell gave her a blank stare. She was about to answer, when two church members who had sung in Paulina's choir interrupted her.

"Hi, ladies," said Ms. Maddox.

"Hello!" said LaTrell and Carmen.

"I overheard you both talking about the Fall Festival. LaTrell, I really wish you would give it some thought. You know your mother would want you to participate," said Ms. Maddox.

Suddenly, LaTrell became very aggravated with Ms. Maddox's comment. She was tired of people bringing Paulina into these situations, using Paulina to persuade LaTrell or Daryl to participate in church activities.

How did Ms. Maddox or anyone else know what Paulina wanted for LaTrell? After all, Paulina wasn't around to ask or speak for herself. The more LaTrell thought about it, the angrier she became, and she had to bite her lip to keep from speaking her mind. She was so happy when Daryl called her name.

"I'll give it some thought, Ms. Maddox," LaTrell said, wasting no time waving goodbye. She quickly turned to join Daryl and Luis. They were finally heading home.

During dinner that night, Daryl ran his mouth, as usual. LaTrell was still pretty bothered by Ms. Maddox's comment. Distracted by her emotions, she picked over her food.

"What's wrong, sweet pea? You aren't hungry?" asked Luis.

"Not really," LaTrell said.

"Well, what's wrong?" Luis asked.

The only sound that could be heard was Daryl smacking on his food. To hear LaTrell better, he chewed in slow motion.

LaTrell put down her fork and let out a long sigh.

"Well, after church, in the multipurpose room . . ." LaTrell stopped talking and looked over at Luis.

"Mm-hmm," Luis said, prompting her to continue.

"I was talking to Carmen, when Ms. Maddox came over, stating that she'd overheard Carmen asking me when I was going to start attending Junior Rubies meetings again. She went on to say that Mama would want me to. That comment made me angry. I don't like when people say, 'Your mama would have wanted it that way,' unless they know for sure. It's like some people expect me to be like Mama, and I don't like how that makes me feel," LaTrell said, as her eyes filled with tears.

"Her comment made you that angry?" Luis asked.

"It's too much pressure. I may not want to do some of the things that Mama did at the church," LaTrell said.

"What are some of the things that you think you *would* like to do in the church?" Luis asked.

"I would like to serve on the Usher Board and not sing in the junior choir. Since Mama was involved with the music ministry, I don't want anyone to think I'm supposed to try to start playing the piano or singing in every choir, either. And I'm not even sure I want to stay active with the Junior Rubies," LaTrell said.

The Junior Rubies were designed for girls

between the ages of eleven and seventeen. Their activities were centered on mission work, life skills, and building character.

"I think that's fair," Luis said.

Luis turned to Daryl and asked, "Do you feel like you've been under pressure since your mother died? Has anyone ever commented to you that your mother would have wanted you to do something?"

"I felt more pressure when Mama was alive," Daryl said, licking his fingers.

"What do you mean?" Luis asked.

"There were a few times when Mama would want me to play the drums with her and the choir. Sometimes I just didn't feel like it. I've always felt like if I wanted to do anything, I should enjoy it. If I'm made to do it, then I will have an attitude about it. Now I feel a little guilty about the times I didn't play the drums for Mama and the choir. I hope she has forgiven me, though," Daryl said, ending in a whisper.

"It's okay, son. Your mother was a forgiving person. No one is perfect," Luis said.

"I'm glad we're having this talk. I wasn't aware that you both were experiencing this. I know that as children, you don't want to disrespect adults. However, it's okay to speak up for yourself and do it in a respectful manner," Luis said, looking at LaTrell, then Daryl.

Luis went on to say, "I don't want you two ever to feel forced to do anything because someone says your mom would want you to do it. Remember that you have choices. If an opportunity becomes available and you know that you would put great energy into it, then go for it. If not, then you need to let people know that you don't want to take part in anything that you're not interested in or going to put forth any effort toward. It wouldn't be fair to you or them."

"I know, right?" LaTrell said.

"Some may be disappointed, but I think they would appreciate your honesty," Luis said with a matter-of-fact expression.

"Okay," LaTrell said.

Daryl shook his head in agreement with LaTrell.

That Wednesday, Daryl asked Luis to drop him off at the church. He had decided to be a part of the step show with the Junior Christian Gentlemen group. LaTrell rode along. Since Daryl was making an effort to take part in church activities, LaTrell had decided she would, too.

When they pulled up to the church, LaTrell told Luis to wait for her, because she just wanted to sign up for a committee. Daryl and LaTrell got out of the car and walked inside the church.

"Hey there, little Paulina! Will you be blessing us with your musical talents for the Fall Festival this year?" Mr. Barnett, LaTrell's band teacher, asked, while moving his fingers as if he were playing the flute.

"Huh? Oh, no, no!" LaTrell said, as she felt like a deer caught in headlights. "Maybe next year!"

"I was just kidding. Your sound is getting better. Just keep practicing," Mr. Barnett said, chuckling, as he walked off with the church musicians.

"Okay, I will," LaTrell said.

As LaTrell and Daryl got closer to the multipurpose room, they heard the group stomping their feet and chanting words. Once they entered the room, the group stopped and started giving Daryl high fives and handshakes. They seemed quite excited to see him.

"Daryl, I'm glad you decided to be a part of the show, lil' man," Shad said, smiling.

While Daryl was in the midst of this exciting greeting, LaTrell wandered over to the sign-up sheets.

"Wait here for a second. I want to speak with you and the other two gentlemen you had a run-in with the other Sunday," Shad said.

Shad got the attention of Jason and Chris, and they both walked over.

"All right, guys, listen. I heard about the situation that happened between you three. I'm all for joking around, but you must know when to stop. I want to remind you that the Junior Christian Gentlemen group is not about making fun of or insulting one another. Instead, we uplift and bond with one another through the good and bad times," Shad said.

"I didn't mean to make you upset, Daryl," Jason said.

"Yeah, me either. I was just playing," said Chris.

"Thanks for apologizing, boys. So, are we good?" Shad asked.

All three boys said yes. They shook hands and joined the remaining group members.

After weeks of planning, practice, and preparation the day of the Fall Festival finally arrived. The field outside the church was decorated with hay, large banners, streamers, pumpkins, and big lights. There were activities for all ages. The smell of food filled the air. Kids were running to get on the moonwalks. Some adults were in line to participate in the pie-eating and dunk contests. Most of the crowd was sitting in front of the stage under a big tent, waiting on the talent and fashion shows.

As soon as the sun set, the spotlights facing the stage became brighter. The crowd started cheering. A tall, dark figure approached the microphone. LaTrell moved closer to get a better look. Then she heard the voice. It was Reverend Hopkins.

"Good evening, church family and friends. I want to thank each of you for coming out to take part in the festivities. Please be sure to visit the bake-sale table and the game booths. I can't wait to see the talent that we have here tonight. Now, without further ado, put your hands together for our first act, the Junior Christian Gentlemen!" Reverend Hopkins said.

The sounds of applause echoed throughout the festival. Daryl and the Junior Christian Gentlemen looked cool in their outfits. The group began chanting and doing unique steps using their hands, legs, and feet. When they finished, the crowd erupted with excitement.

"What a way to start the show," said Reverend Hopkins, as he got ready to announce another act.

LaTrell was so happy for them. *Mama would have been so proud of Daryl*, she thought. She walked over to the bake-sale table, and just as she got there, she heard a voice say, "Is that Ms. LaTrell?"

LaTrell turned around slowly and said, "Yes."

It was Alexis and her mother. Alexis was another Junior Rubies member, around LaTrell's age.

"Oh, hey!" LaTrell said.

"Girl, we had to find you before the night was over with. Did you make those sack cakes?" asked Alexis.

"Yep!" LaTrell said, nodding her head.

"Well, they were just delicious," Alexis's mom blurted out. "Your mother taught you well."

Before LaTrell knew it, there was a domino effect. One of the deacons passed by and overheard the conversation. He stopped to tell LaTrell how much he liked the sack cakes and said that he would like for LaTrell to make a batch for his family for Thanksgiving.

LaTrell could see Chandler out the corner of her eye, holding two sack cakes in his left hand and eating one with his right hand. Then three members from Paulina's choir gathered around to congratulate LaTrell on a job well done. For the rest of the night, LaTrell received compliments on the sack cakes. She couldn't stop smiling and blushing.

Chandler walked toward LaTrell, chewing like a cow with crumbs around his mouth.

"LaTrell, if there was a crime for making good desserts, you would be in jail without a doubt," Chandler said with his mouth full.

"Chandler, you are so silly. You better stop eating so many sweets before you get a stomachache," LaTrell said, shaking her head.

"Too late. My stomach started hurting a while ago. I'm just fighting through it because I'm not finished eating. My grandma said I better eat as much as I can, because she isn't cooking," Chandler said, and walked off.

September 30
Hi Mama! I did it again. I made sack cakes for the church Fall Festival. A lot of people enjoyed eating them. I think I'm kinda getting the hang of making them! I felt a little guilty for not wanting to do anything with music, but I'm glad I can keep your memory alive with the baking skills you passed down to me. I miss you.

Chapter 2 Questions

1. Have you ever been pressured to fill the shoes of a loved one who is no longer around?

2. Have you ever regretted doing something you should not have done? Or is there something you regret not doing because you failed to speak up?

3. We all have an inner voice, which is also referred to as our gut instinct. Can you name a time when your inner voice kicked in? Did you listen? Or did you ignore it?

Three

The Party Doesn't Stop

Daryl's birthday was in a few days. Luis and LaTrell exchanged ideas all week long.

One night, as they all sat at the dinner table, LaTrell asked Luis, "Since Daryl had a good time at the Fall Festival with the Junior Christian Gentlemen Crusade, why don't we invite them to do paintball?"

Luis turned and looked at LaTrell. "Sounds like a plan to me. What do you think, Daryl?" he asked.

Daryl pumped his fist in the air. "Ooh-wee . . . this is going to be fun," he said, while smacking his food. He paused and then asked, "Are you going to send a text to all of their parents? Or an e-mail?"

"Hunh? I don't know how to use that stuff, son. I was going to buy invitations and have you pass them out when you get to church and school," Luis said.

"Oh, come on, Dad. Boys my age don't give out invitations. Besides, I would lose major cool points for that," Daryl said, looking offended.

"How about I just call each of the parents, then?" Luis asked.

"That sounds more like it," Daryl said, looking relieved. He walked off toward his bedroom.

LaTrell smiled, shook her head, and followed behind him.

When Daryl got to his room, LaTrell stopped in the doorway.

"Who are you going to invite?" LaTrell asked.

I'm going to ask Jason, Chris, Alex, Trevor, and Big Russell," Daryl said, counting on his fingers.

"Big Russell? Wait, he's my age," LaTrell said.

"I know, but he's still fun to hang out with," Daryl said.

LaTrell gave Daryl a strange look. "What do you want for your birthday?" she asked.

Daryl shrugged his shoulders. "What do you think Mama would get me this year?" he asked.

"Well, since you're turning nine, she would probably buy you a gift card from your favorite store," LaTrell said.

"Yeah, you're probably right. It just feels so weird not having her around to celebrate our birthdays," Daryl said, looking at the floor. Then he looked up, his eyes beaming with excitement, and said, "Hey! Remember the big parties Mama always threw us?"

"You bet I do. One thing about Mama, she knew how to celebrate big," LaTrell said, smiling.

Daryl nodded in agreement.

"I loved her surprises. Mama always gave us the small gift first, and then, out of nowhere, she would place a bigger gift in front of you," Daryl said, holding his hands far apart, as if he were holding a box.

"Yep, she sure would." LaTrell laughed, cupping her mouth.

"Mama made our favorite cakes, too!" Daryl said, looking at LaTrell as if he had just thought of an idea. "Do you think you can make me that pineapple upside-down cake like Mama used to?" he asked hesitantly.

"You want *me* to make a cake like that?" LaTrell asked, pointing at herself.

"Please," Daryl said, dragging the word out for a few seconds.

"Okay, I will check in Mama's recipe box to look over the ingredients. I don't know if it will taste like Mama's, but I will do my best," LaTrell said.

"Well, you do a great job with the sack cakes; I think you'll do a great job with this cake, too. Boy, all this talk about cake is making my mouth water," Daryl said, licking his lips.

Then Daryl's smiled quickly disappeared. LaTrell saw his face and immediately stopped laughing. "What's wrong?" she asked.

"I miss Mama a lot," Daryl said, looking at LaTrell.

LaTrell walked toward Daryl and put her hand around his shoulders.

"I know, little bro. We all miss her. The good thing is, we can always laugh about the good memories she left us," LaTrell said. "Besides, I think Dad is, like, the bomb parent!" she added.

"Yeah, Dad is the number-one guy right now. I'm glad we still have him. Some of my friends have never met their father or haven't seen them in a long time," Daryl said.

"What if we never knew who our dad was and Mama left? Who would take us in? Where would we go?" Daryl said, with fear in his eyes.

LaTrell looked at Daryl. She finally broke the silence and said, "I'm sure that Dad isn't going anywhere, and we will always have each other."

LaTrell moved slightly in front of him and slowly raised her right hand to give Daryl a high five.

"You're right. Me, you, and Dad are like the Three Amigos," Daryl said.

Later that evening, LaTrell went to Paulina's recipe box, which was kept in one of the kitchen drawers. She took the top off and began searching for the pineapple upside down-cake recipe.

"Here it is," she said out loud. The index card was titled "Pineapple Upside-Down Cake":

¼ cup butter or margarine
1 cup packed brown sugar
1 can (20 oz.) pineapple slices in juice, drained, juice reserved
1 jar (6 oz.) maraschino cherries without stems, drained
1 box Betty Crocker Super Moist yellow cake mix
Vegetable oil and eggs called for on cake-mix box

1. Preheat the oven to 350°F and combine the ingredients step by step.
2. Next, in a 9 x 13–inch pan, melt butter in oven. Sprinkle brown sugar evenly over butter. Place pineapple slices on top of brown sugar mixture. Then pour the batter on top of it. Lift the cake pan up a few inches with both hands and drop it on the counter a few times to get the air bubbles out. Finally, place the cake inside the oven and set the timer for 45 minutes.

She looked over the recipe list. *This doesn't look too hard*, LaTrell said to herself. She made a grocery list of the items Luis needed to buy.

Luis was reclining in his chair as he watched the evening news in the den. LaTrell walked in and placed a piece of paper torn from a notepad on the side table.

"What's that?" Luis asked.

LaTrell sat down and let out a loud sigh. "It's a grocery list. Daryl wants me to make a pineapple upside-down cake like Mama made for his birthday each year," LaTrell said, giving Luis a doubtful look.

Luis's eyes grew wide. "He does?"

"Yes, and he's serious," LaTrell said, nodding her head up and down. "I think this will make Daryl feel better."

"What do you mean?" Luis asked.

"Well, we had a talk after dinner and he said he really misses Mama, especially when birthdays come around," LaTrell said.

Luis's face grew concerned, and he lifted the handle on the side of his recliner to bring the chair upright.

"He seemed better after our talk. I think he was just having a moment," LaTrell said.

"Thank you for letting me know. I'll check on

him before I go to bed," Luis said.

LaTrell left the den and disappeared around the corner. Luis looked down at the list again. "Humph, LaTrell is going to attempt to make this cake, hunh?" he said with a half smile.

He placed the list on the side table next to a picture of him and Paulina from their fifteenth wedding anniversary. Luis picked up the frame and gazed at the photograph. He remembered that day vividly: he and Paulina had attended a Gladys Knight concert and eaten dinner at a seafood restaurant on the beach to celebrate. One of the things he missed most about Paulina was her companionship; they had done a lot together, like attend birthday celebrations, weddings, and travel.

We sure had some good times together, Paulina, Luis said to himself, shaking his head. *I wish we could have done more. It looks like all of us are missing you in different ways. They say we aren't supposed to question God. To be honest, I don't think there is ever a good time to say goodbye. Just know you are missed, Paulina.* Luis looked once more at the picture as he set it back on the side table.

LaTrell decided to make Daryl's cake the evening before his birthday. There was no school for students on Friday, in observance of Columbus Day. Daryl's birthday party would be held on Saturday.

After LaTrell washed the dishes, Daryl swept the kitchen while she assembled the ingredients on the counter.

After Daryl put the broom and dustpan away, he washed his hands. Then, as if he were a hypnotist, he said, "LaTrell, before you start, I want you to close your eyes and picture Mama making this cake."

"Daryl, will you get out?" LaTrell said, cutting her eyes at him and pointing with a wooden spoon.

"All right, I'm going. But I'll be back in thirty minutes to check on you," he said, patting LaTrell on the shoulder as he walked out of the kitchen.

"Well, I might as well join you," Luis said chuckling.

Luis and Daryl went into the den to watch a few reruns of *Everybody Hates Chris*.

Luis took off his glasses and rubbed his eyes. Then he repositioned his glasses and cleared his throat.

"Daryl, is everything okay? LaTrell mentioned to me yesterday that you were feeling a little down," Luis said.

"Yes," Daryl nodded, without making eye contact. Then he slowly turned his head to face Luis and continued, "Yeah, I'm okay. I just think about Mom more during birthdays and the holidays. She liked to celebrate big. Ever since she left, I've been afraid that we won't have parties anymore or go out to dinner."

"Why would you think that?" Luis asked.

"Because Mama planned everything and we just helped out and joined in the fun," Daryl said.

"You're right—she did do all of the planning—but I like to have fun, too. I don't see any reason to stop having celebrations just because Mom is no longer with us. We will celebrate until we decide as a family to stop," Luis said.

"You mean it?" Daryl asked.

"Of course I do. I don't think your mother would want it any other way. She started the tradition, so we will carry it on," Luis said with confidence.

Daryl let out a deep sigh of relief.

In the kitchen, the timer rang loudly. LaTrell turned off the oven and carefully removed the cake to let it rest for a few minutes. Next, she took a small rubber spatula out of a drawer and ran it around the edges of the cake to loosen it from the sides of the pan. She had seen Paulina do this with most of her cakes.

Here goes nothing, LaTrell said to herself. She placed the cake plate on top of the cake pan and flipped it upside down with two hands. The cake slid out slowly and landed perfectly on the plate. The gooey mixture from the bottom of the cake pan followed behind.

Luis and Daryl got up from their seats and stood on both sides of LaTrell to watch.

"Oh, I almost forgot to add the cherries," LaTrell said, placing cherries all over the cake.

The cake was finally ready to be eaten. Sitting on a tall glass plate, it looked like a piece of jewelry. The glaze on the cake resembled shimmering lights, and the pineapple rings looked like miniature sunsets in a desert.

Luis began whistling as he reached for plates and forks. Anytime he whistled, it meant he was in a happy mood.

Luis and Daryl remained standing as they each took their first bite.

"Yes!" Daryl said, and broke out into a dance.

"Mmm-mmm," Luis said, shaking his head.

"So, does that mean y'all like it?" LaTrell asked, with one eyebrow up.

"LaTrell, you have another winner on your hands," Luis said, before taking another bite.

"You mean it?" LaTrell asked.

Luis and Daryl both shook their heads, their mouths full of cake.

Daryl finished chewing and said, "You know what? After Mama died, I didn't think I would ever eat another homemade pineapple upside-down cake for my birthday. Thanks for making this cake, LaTrell. I guess you really were paying attention." He took another bite.

"Hey, I can read directions," LaTrell said, with her hand on her hip.

"Yeah, but baking is more then reading words; it takes skill. You most definitely inherited that from Paulina," Luis said.

"Aw, thank you, Daddy," LaTrell said, blushing.

Daryl finished scraping the crumbs off his plate and surprised LaTrell by saying, "I'm so happy right now that I'm going to wash dishes for you."

LaTrell looked at Daryl with a shocked face.

"Well, you don't have to tell me twice," she said, hurrying out of the kitchen as if she were chasing a fly.

Luis and Daryl held their stomachs, bursting with laughter.

October 12

Hi Mama! I seem to be getting the hang of baking deserts. Daryl asked me to make his favorite cake. Can you guess what it is? Yep! Pineapple upside-down cake. I made it for him yesterday. Dad and Daryl really liked it too. I must admit that I was hesitant at first. I wanted the cake to taste the way you made it. Mama, you kind of messed it up for me, because you did everything so perfect (smile). I think baking deserts is fun, but I'm not you. Comparing my baking skills to yours can be stressful. I wish everyone understood that. Daryl's party is tomorrow. I'll let you know how it turns out. Miss you!

The next morning, Daryl was the first person up. He was excited because today was his birthday. Since he hadn't had a party last year, he wondered how this one would turn out.

As Daryl ate his cereal, all types of questions crossed his mind. *Will everyone show up? Will they like paintball? Will I get a lot of gifts?* All that wondering made Daryl's excitement turn quickly into nervousness.

Daryl's thinking was soon interrupted when Luis entered the kitchen.

"I see the birthday boy has gotten his day started already," Luis said.

"I couldn't sleep. I can't wait until the party," Daryl said.

"Me neither; it's going to be fun," Luis said.

"LaTrell isn't up yet?" Daryl asked.

"No, LaTrell is sleeping in a little longer. I think all the concentration on baking the cake wore her out," Luis said, laughing.

Daryl smiled back.

"I'm going to eat a quick breakfast. I need to go to the store and pick up your cupcakes and a few other items for the party," Luis said. "Would you like to come?"

Daryl thought for a minute, then said, "No, I need to see which outfit I'm going to wear to my party."

"Which *outfit*? You're going to be wearing paintball protective gear most of the time. Who's going to notice what else you have on?" Luis asked.

"Dad, I have to look fresh wherever I go,"

Daryl said, with a matter-of-fact facial expression.

"Okay, Daryl," Luis said, shaking his head.

While Luis ran his errands, LaTrell finally awoke. She passed by Daryl's room on the way to the bathroom.

"Hey, LaTrell, when you finish in there, can you help me choose a shirt to wear with my gray jeans?" Daryl asked from his room.

LaTrell raised her hand to acknowledge Daryl. After getting herself together, she walked into his room to find him holding up two shirts.

Daryl turned to LaTrell. "Which one?" he asked.

LaTrell pointed to the light gray Sean John button-down shirt.

"Why did you choose that one?" Daryl asked.

"Because the color is a lighter shade and pairs nicely with your jeans," LaTrell said.

Daryl looked at LaTrell and said, "Not only do you bake like Mama, you got her taste in style, too," Daryl said, smiling.

"You are so crazy, Daryl," LaTrell said, walking out of his room.

Since Daryl had chosen his outfit, LaTrell decided to go ahead and get dressed. She knew paintball was a messy game, so she put on a pair of jeans, a pink-and-white top, and sneakers.

Not long after that, Luis opened the door, his arms

were full. LaTrell walked quickly alongside him to the dining room table to take some of the stuff out of his hands.

Luis put a box of cupcakes on the table. They were shaped like the number 9 and frosted with blue, white, and yellow buttercream icing.

"Oh, those look good. I need to take a picture before the boys get to them," LaTrell said.

"That's a good idea." Luis said.

Daryl walked in like he was one of the cool teenagers in the neighborhood.

"Somebody is sharp today," Luis said, smiling.

"What's that smell?" LaTrell asked, sniffing the air.

"Oh, you smell me? I smell good, hunh? I put a little dab of Dad's cologne on my chest," Daryl said, with a proud smile.

"Your chest?" LaTrell asked.

"No, son, you're supposed to put a small dab on both of your wrists and behind both ears," Luis said, smiling.

"I don't think you should have done that!" LaTrell said.

"Why not?" Daryl said.

"Because your cologne is going to give away where you're hiding during the paintball game," LaTrell said.

As she started walking away, Daryl looked at Luis and said, "Oh, I forgot about that."

Luis smirked and said, "We can see that."

LaTrell came back with a camera. She opened the box to take a picture of the cupcakes and then reclosed it.

"Ooh, those cupcakes look delicious," Daryl said, licking his lips, as usual.

"All right, are you all ready to go? I want to get there a little early, before the parents drop off their kids," Luis said.

"You know I stay ready," Daryl said, straightening out his shirt.

LaTrell and Daryl grabbed the balloons, and Luis carried the cupcakes to the car.

During the drive, LaTrell noticed that the sun was shining more brightly than usual. She smiled, thinking that maybe this was Paulina's way of being present for Daryl's birthday.

As Luis got closer, he turned down the radio and said, "Are you guys ready to have some fun?"

Daryl yelled, "Yeah!"

LaTrell let out a "woohoo!"

Luis laughed. "You two are funny," he said.

Luis pulled into the parking lot. Daryl stuck his head out of the window to get a closer look. Even before Luis cut the engine, Daryl had one foot out of the car. He grabbed all of the balloons and walked ahead. He was in such a hurry to get inside, he didn't notice LaTrell holding his presents.

Once they got inside, the party host greeted them and showed them their table. It was decorated with a party tablecloth, paper plates, and cups. Luis and LaTrell took a few balloons from Daryl and tied them around the chairs.

Soon after that, Daryl's party guests began to arrive. LaTrell noticed Big Russell getting out of a car playing loud bass music and filled with cigarette smoke. He gave the driver and passenger fist pounds and proceeded into the building.

Who in the world are those boys? LaTrell said to herself, wrinkling her nose.

When everyone was finally in place, Daryl smiled from ear to ear.

"Would you all like to eat now, or wait until you finish your paintball game?" Luis asked.

"After the paintball game!" the boys yelled.

"Okay, then follow me," the hostess said.

Everyone followed the hostess into a big, open field filled with large objects, like tires, door frames, old cars, and small buildings. At the entrance to the field, the hostess explained the rules and handed each person a pair of face goggles, a protective jumpsuit, and a paintball gun.

All of the players were ready to begin. Within the first ten minutes, LaTrell's left leg was covered in red paint. She looked up and saw that Luis had fired the shot.

"Thanks a lot, Dad!" LaTrell yelled.

"You're welcome, sweetie!" Luis yelled back, as he ran to hide behind a car.

LaTrell was kind of glad she got out first. She had not planned on getting sweaty and having smashed hair. While she waited for their game to finish, she returned the equipment and went inside to get the camera; then she sat on the bench and snapped pictures. Luis seemed to be just as competitive as the boys. "Go, Dad, go!" LaTrell yelled.

A few minutes later, the party guests were squirted with loud-colored paint, one after another. Luis turned in his equipment and joined LaTrell and the others on the bench. Daryl was determined to win and pass the objectives of the game by capturing the flag. His determination paid off.

The boys high-fived one another on a good game.

"I thought that game would never end," Daryl said, putting his gray shirt back on. He had taken it off and kept on only his white undershirt.

Everyone agreed.

Back inside, the boys went to the restroom to wash their hands.

"Hey, what are y'all doing for Halloween?" Big Russell asked.

The boys shrugged their shoulders.

"Well, y'all should come to my block. We get a lot of candy," Big Russell said, with a smirk.

A few of the boys gave Russell a funny look. They knew that block was known for high crime activity.

"How many adult chaperones come along?" Daryl asked.

"Oh, don't worry about all of that. There will be enough," Russell said, making a basket shot with the paper napkin.

Daryl looked at the rest of the boys to see what they were thinking.

"I'll ask my dad," said Daryl.

The other boys agreed that they would also ask their parents. They quickly exited the bathroom to join the party.

As Daryl and the boys laughed and joked about their performance on the paintball field, Luis asked, "Did you all have fun?"

"Yes," everyone said.

"I'm going to ask my mom if I can have my party here," Jason said.

"Glad to hear," Luis said.

After they finished off two more rounds of pizza and drinks, the boys were ready for cupcakes.

Luis took the sheet of cupcakes out of the box and placed it in front of Daryl. The hostess lit a number 9 candle and led the group in singing "Happy Birthday." LaTrell had the camera in position, ready to snap.

"Make a wish, Daryl," LaTrell said after the song ended.

Daryl closed his eyes for a few seconds and blew the candle out with a great big smile. LaTrell took that picture and more of Daryl having a good time with his friends. When the last picture was snapped, she realized that Paulina used to do the same thing: capture special moments.

Later on that evening, Daryl sat on the floor in the den and arranged the gift cards he had gotten, in order from the highest to the lowest amount.

"Well, did you have fun today?" Luis asked.

"Yep! Too much fun. Thanks, Dad," Daryl said, smiling at Luis. "Oh, Dad! Can I go trick-or-treating with Big Russell on his block for Halloween?" Daryl continued. "He says there will be enough adults. And this will be the first time I go with friends."

LaTrell came around the corner just in time to hear Daryl's question.

"No way!" LaTrell blurted out, before Luis could answer the question.

"LaTrell, I didn't ask you!" Daryl snapped.

"Dad, Big Russell lives on one of the roughest blocks in the neighborhood. It's not safe over there," LaTrell said, looking at Luis, with her right hand on her hip.

"So what, LaTrell? That doesn't mean anything bad is going to happen to me," Daryl said.

"LaTrell does have a point, Daryl. Just last week, there was a drug bust and a few home burglaries. I don't know about this. Maybe I need to come along," Luis said, giving him a concerned look.

"But, Dad, I'm not a baby anymore. You don't have to go with me everywhere. LaTrell, why don't you just mind your business!" Daryl said, as he stomped off to his room.

LaTrell and Luis looked at each other in silence. They had never seen Daryl so upset. LaTrell raised her hands to massage both sides of her head and went to her room. After that blowup, she felt like she needed a nap. Not to mention that the Wigginses had been on the go the last two weekends, first for their church's Fall Festival last week, and now for Daryl's birthday.

October 13

Hi Mama! Daryl had a blast at his paintball party. He misses you so much! Dad and I got him two gifts, just like you used to give. He was really surprised. After spending a day with six boys, I'm glad I have only one brother. We didn't think we would pull it off, but we did. But now Daryl is mad at us. He wants to go trick-or-treating on Big Russell's block. Do you remember him from my fifth-grade class in elementary school? Mama, you know that block is not safe! What's worse is that Daryl wants to go by himself. I don't feel right about Daryl going, Mama. And anyway, I think Daryl is too young to be hanging around Big Russell. Dad said he'll think about it. What in the world does he have to think about? Can you whisper in Dad's ear to get him to make the right decision? Love you!

Chapter 3 Questions

1. Does your family have any traditions (e.g., birthdays, family dinners, game night) that have continued in the absence of a loved one? Do the events feel the same? How do the traditions feel different?

2. Daryl seems to be intrigued by Big Russell. In chapter 1, we saw how much LaTrell admired Peaches. Have you ever hung around friends older than you? If so, what did you admire about them?

3. When someone like a parent or an older sibling voices an objection to something you want to do, what do you think is going on? Are they trying to take away your independence and fun? Or is it something else?

<u>Four</u>

Secrets

The days leading up to Halloween intensified Daryl's sweet tooth. He knew what types of candies he wanted. After Daryl's blowup with LaTrell over his wanting to go trick-or-treating with Big Russell, he finally calmed down and slowly came around to being his usual self again. Daryl had already assumed and accepted that Luis wouldn't let him trick-or-treat with Big Russell. What mattered most to him was being able to dress up as a character and get candy.

"LaTrell, does this look okay?" Daryl asked, standing in her doorway.

"Who are you supposed to be dressed up as?" LaTrell asked, giving him a confused look.

"You mean you can't tell? I'm Drake, the hip-hop artist," Daryl said, hands raised.

Daryl had on a white shirt with black writing that said STARTED FROM THE BOTTOM, a pair of blue jeans, a black jacket, and black high-top sneakers. He had linked jumbo paper clips to make two big chain necklaces.

"Ahhh, I see it now. Yes, you *are* dressed up like Drake," LaTrell said, nodding her head.

"Good! Now Halloween just needs to hurry up and get here," Daryl said excitedly, walking back to his room.

***

The night before Halloween, the Wiggins's had dinner and listened to Daryl run his mouth, as usual.

"Daryl, I had some time to think about what you asked. I've decided to let you go trick-or-treating with Big Russell, on one condition: an adult must go with you. I figured it's okay to let you go places without me from time to time," Luis said, looking at Daryl with a serious face.

Luis's answer caught LaTrell and Daryl off guard.

"Really, Dad?" Daryl said, slowly raising himself out of his seat, looking shocked.

"Say what!" LaTrell blurted, as she spit out her drink. "Dad, you can't be serious."

"Goodness, why are you and Daryl so surprised? I don't think I'm *that* strict," Luis said.

Luis caught LaTrell and Daryl looking at him as if he had three heads. "On the other hand, maybe

I am," he said, shrugging his shoulders.

"Thanks, Dad. You rock!" Daryl said, smiling as he got up from the table.

"You're welcome, son," Luis said, following behind him.

LaTrell remained at the table and let out a long sigh.

***

Finally, one of people's favorite days of the year, when everyone from small kids to adults gets to dress up as their favorite character, arrived: Halloween. Daryl couldn't wait for the school day to be over. LaTrell couldn't wait, either—but she was one of the few people who did not look forward to Halloween. To her, it was just a day that glorified a whole lot of spookiness.

As soon as Daryl got home, he fixed himself a snack and called his friends who had attended his party to see if they were going with Big Russell. To Daryl's surprise, they all said no.

The last person Daryl called was Big Russell.

"What's up?" Big Russell said when he answered.

"Hey, Big Russ, what time should I come over to go trick-or-treating?" Daryl asked.

"Uh, come over around 7:00 p.m.," Big Russell said.

"Okay. And will there be an adult coming along with us? Because that's the only way my dad will let me come," Daryl said

"No, we never have adults with us. My mother works at night anyway. But I can have my neighbor act as my aunt so that you can come," Big Russell said, without hesitation.

"You mean you get to go trick-or-treating by yourself?" asked Daryl.

"Dude, I'm not a baby. Plus, everyone on my street knows one another. Don't worry. My plan will work," Big Russell said.

"I sure hope so. See you at seven," Daryl said, trying not to sound doubtful.

It was bad enough that none of Daryl's best buddies were going, and now he had learned that he would be trick-or-treating without an adult present. *There's no way I'm going to tell my dad about this*, Daryl said to himself. He wanted to hang out with Big Russell so badly that he was willing to keep a secret from Luis—something he had never done before.

Later that evening, Luis came home from work. Daryl, who was already dressed in his costume, met Luis at the front door.

"How did I know you would already be dressed, son?" Luis said with a chuckle. "What time should I drop you off at Big Russell's house?"

"He wants me there at seven o'clock," Daryl said.

LaTrell overheard Luis and Daryl talking as she warmed up dinner in the kitchen. She glanced around the corner to get a good look at Daryl and shook her head. LaTrell still couldn't believe Luis was allowing Daryl to go.

The closer it got to seven o'clock, the more nervous Daryl seemed. He realized there would be no Jason, Chris, Alex, or Trevor. He was going to be hanging out with Big Russell by himself.

Luis and Daryl arrived at Big Russell's house on time. The block had one streetlight, which flickered off and on. Each house seemed to have at least one nonworking car sitting on bricks or missing a part. Daryl looked worried, but he didn't want Luis to see.

"This block sure looks different from ours," Daryl said.

"You got that right. Are you sure you want to go trick-or-treating over here?" Luis asked, trying not to change his mind.

Daryl looked around again. "Yes, I'm sure," he said slowly.

Luis was about to ask another question, when the front door of Big Russell's house opened. Big

Russell and a woman appeared and made their way toward Luis's car.

"Hi, Mr. Wiggins, this is my Aunt Cynthia. She's going to come with us," Big Russell said, pointing to the woman and smirking.

"Hi," the woman said, waving to Luis and smiling. "Daryl is in good hands."

"Well, that's good to know," Luis said. "I will be back to pick you up at eight fifteen," he said to Daryl.

Daryl nodded his head in agreement.

"Okay, son, be safe and keep up with Big Russell," Luis said, as he got back in the car.

As Luis drove away, he got a funny feeling in his gut. *Well, I guess my boy is growing up*, he said to himself. Daryl watched until Luis disappeared around the corner. He turned around and saw Aunt Cynthia going inside the same house that three teenagers were exiting. Two males and one female, whom he recognized from playing pickup basketball around the neighborhood, joined them. They all had on shorts, T-shirts, and different scary masks hanging from their necks. Daryl looked down at himself and back at them. He was the only one dressed in full costume. He also noticed they all had grocery bags to collect their candy, and he was carrying an orange pumpkin by the handle.

Daryl became a little embarrassed and didn't think he looked as cool as the others.

"Okay, let's go," Big Russell said.

The nervousness Daryl had felt earlier now turned into full-blown fear. He wondered what in the world he had gotten himself into.

***

Meanwhile, back at the house, LaTrell was busy passing out candy to excited trick-or-treaters. Luis sat in the den, watching TV. He kept looking at his watch and counting the minutes until eight fifteen. LaTrell later joined Luis in the den. She plopped down and curled her feet up on the couch. LaTrell wanted to ask a few questions but decided just to sit in silence instead. She could tell Luis wasn't in the mood to talk anyway. He seemed anxious, as he quickly flipped through the channels and kept looking at his watch.

Around eight o'clock, Luis couldn't wait any longer. He hopped up from the recliner and grabbed his keys and wallet.

"I'll be back. I'm going to wait on Daryl," Luis said over his shoulder.

Luis pulled up to Big Russell's house and noticed the woman he had met as Aunt Cynthia sitting on the front porch, talking on the phone.

"Did you all finish up earlier than expected?" Luis asked from the car.

"Oh, I didn't go," she said, waving Luis off as she continued talking on the phone.

All of a sudden, Luis felt anger raging inside him. Then a voice called out, "Hey, Dad!"

Luis got out of his car and walked toward Daryl and the rest of the group, highlighted by the streetlight.

"Big Russell, you told me that your Aunt Cynthia was going to go along with you all. But she didn't. Did you tell me a lie?" Luis asked, standing with both hands on his hips.

Big Russell dropped his head and nodded his head up and down.

"Daryl, were you in on this lie?" Luis asked.

"Yes," Daryl replied, ashamed.

"I am very disappointed. I trusted you two. Daryl, get in the car," Luis said, pointing angrily at the car.

Daryl didn't even say goodbye to Big Russell and the others. He silently turned toward the car and got inside. The ride home seemed like the longest five minutes of Daryl's life. He couldn't wait to get in the house, get out of his costume, and take a bath, but he was mostly concerned about what kind of punishment Luis would give him.

LaTrell knew something was wrong when

Daryl didn't come inside the house bragging about his time with Big Russell. In fact, he didn't even make eye contact with her. Instead, Daryl brushed right past her and continued to his room. LaTrell then turned to Luis. His eyes and facial expression could've been a Halloween mask. She quickly shut and locked the front door.

When Daryl finished his bath, he slowly opened the bathroom door to see if Luis was around. Once he determined the coast was clear, he made a dash to his bedroom. To his surprise, LaTrell was sitting on the edge of his bed, waiting on him.

"What happened?' LaTrell asked, her hands slightly extended.

Daryl sighed. "I made a big mistake," he said, looking at the floor. "I told Dad that an adult was going to come along with us, but I knew ahead of time that no adult was coming.

"You mean you wanted to go trick-or-treating over there so bad that you lied?" LaTrell asked.

"Was it worth it?" a deep voice asked, peering in the doorway to Daryl's room.

Luis had been standing outside of Daryl's room, listening to their conversation. Daryl's heart began to beat quickly. He shook his head no.

"You didn't think I was going to find out?" Luis asked.

"I was hoping you wouldn't," Daryl said, still not making eye contact.

"Daryl, this has me a little worried. You've never lied or done anything like this before. Now I wish I had listened to your sister. Tell me, why were you so eager to trick-or-treat with Big Russell?" Luis asked.

"Because I think he's cool. And I thought if other boys my age saw me hanging out with him, they would think I was cool, too," Daryl said.

"Hmph!" Luis said, with one eyebrow raised. It had never occurred to him that Daryl wanted to fit in and be cool. "I see. But there's plenty of time to be cool. You just turned nine. I understand that you're not a baby, but at some events an adult needs to be present to keep order or prevent harm. Do you understand what I'm saying?" Luis asked.

Daryl nodded his head.

"If you want me to trust you, lying isn't going to help. If I tell you no, you have to trust that it's for a good reason," Luis said.

Daryl lifted his head and finally made eye contact with Luis. "I'm sorry, Dad. I won't lie to you again," he said.

"I hope you learned your lesson. Your punishment will be no playing video games and no playing outside with your friends for two weeks,"

Luis said, turning around to walk away.

Daryl hung his head low again. He'd had a small window of hope that the talk would spare him any punishment. He was wrong. LaTrell stood up from where she was sitting on the edge of the bed and gave Daryl a forgiving look before going to her room.

October 31

Hey, Mama! Can you believe Dad ended up letting Daryl go trick-or-treating with Big Russell? Did you forget to whisper the right answer to him? You are not going to believe what your sweet little Daryl did. He lied to Dad about having an adult going trick-or-treating with them. Dad was more upset with Daryl than he was with me when I did the hair color experiment this summer. At least I wasn't put on punishment. You know what, Mama? I know Daryl shouldn't have lied, but I feel sorry for him. I know what it feels like to want to fit in with the cool guys. I did the hair color experiment because I wanted to be cool like Peaches and her crew. Have you ever kept any secrets from Grandma Adela or from us,

Mama? I sure do wish you were here. Love you!

The third weekend of November started off a little chilly and quiet. LaTrell gathered her do-it-yourself nail kit and walked toward the back patio, where she sat and polished her toenails. She hadn't had a professional pedicure since Paulina had gotten sick. Over the last year, LaTrell had improved her polishing skills and added her own creative touches.

LaTrell heard the phone ring a few times, but she didn't move, because she didn't want to mess up her wet toenails. Then Daryl opened the sliding glass door. "Um, your only friend in the whole wide world is on the phone," he said, dangling the phone in front of LaTrell and smirking.

LaTrell reached for the phone without looking at Daryl. She concentrated instead on the design she had made on her big toenail.

"Hello?" LaTrell said.

"Hey, girl! I just called to let you know I'm getting transferred to your technology class on Monday!" the voice on the other end said.

"Hey, Shajuan! Really? Why now? What happened?" LaTrell asked.

"Girl, me and the teacher don't get along at all. She keeps kicking me out or sending me to the office, so my mama requested a class change," Shajuan said, with a slight attitude.

A voice yelled out in Shajaun's background.

"I have to get off this phone and fold some clothes. I'll see you at school on Monday. Oh, and I have a surprise," Shajuan said hurriedly, while giggling.

"A surprise? I can't wait to see. Bye," LaTrell said, as she smiled and hung up the phone.

The next morning, LaTrell couldn't wait to get to school. She would have her best friend in her class. *I wonder what the surprise could be*, she said to herself.

"Good morning, students! Please take a number from the blue basket and sit at the computer that matches your number," Mr. Phillips said, as he stood at the door.

What are we about to do? LaTrell asked herself.

LaTrell was glad to learn more about computers. The previous year, she had been required to complete in-class projects on the computer in only a few of her courses, and those consisted only of typing a few sentences and adding clip art. Mr. Phillips had described the technology class as "vigorous"—a word LaTrell had had to look up. This class was an extension of what she already knew and didn't know existed.

The late bell rang, and Mr. Phillips walked in and closed the door behind him.

"All right, let's get started. I have a lot planned for you all today. From August to October, we have gone over the basic functions of the computer, the different applications of Microsoft Office, saving work, and the school's acceptable-use technology policy for e-mail and social media," Mr. Phillips said, leaning against his desk.

He went on to explain, "Starting today and over the remaining nine weeks, you will be completing a new project. Right now, I would like for each of you to open the folder located to the right of the computer. Be sure to read all the directions first. If you have any questions, raise your hand and I will come to you." Mr. Phillips paused for a moment. Then he said, "You may begin."

LaTrell took a deep breath and let it out slowly. She opened her folder. The first set of directions explained how to set up a school e-mail account step by step. *Hmm, okay. This shouldn't be too hard*, LaTrell said to herself.

"Everyone will follow this format by writing

their first name, then a dot, then their last name, at dadeschools.net. For example, this is how your school e-mail should be written: luke.phillips@student.IvesDairyschools.net," Mr. Phillips wrote on the board. "I'm going to pass a list around for each of you to write down your school e-mail. Remember, you should not share your or your peers' e-mail address with anyone outside this classroom," Mr. Phillips said, looking around.

Suddenly, the door opened and Shajuan walked in. LaTrell beamed with excitement. *Yeah! My friend is here!*

"Well, hi there!" Mr. Phillips said.

"Hello!" Shajuan said, as she gave Mr. Phillips her schedule.

He initialed it and handed it back.

"Go ahead and have a seat at computer eighteen. You will work with Trevor, since you've missed a good deal of the basic training I've taught," Mr. Phillips said.

Shajuan found her seat. After putting down her book bag, she looked over at LaTrell and smiled.

LaTrell smiled back and then returned her attention to the project directions. This would be her first time setting up an e-mail account. Mr. Phillips walked around, checking on students and their progress. He resembled the actor Will Ferrell. Mr. Phillips loved to laugh and tell jokes. The problem was, he was the only one who thought they were funny. Each time he walked past the open window, the breeze blew through his curls like a rake in the grass. Mr. Phillips was also a neat dresser. His slacks had a stiff crease in the pants leg, and his shirts were heavily starched. What LaTrell enjoyed most about Mr. Phillips was that he smelled nice. *I'm going to have to buy my dad some of that cologne*, she thought.

"Okay, students, you have about five minutes until the bell rings. If you are in the middle of your task, make sure you save your work properly. Good job today!" Mr. Phillips said, opening the classroom door.

The bell rang for the next period. LaTrell gathered her things and waited for Shajuan in the hallway. When Shajuan walked past Mr. Phillips, she closed her eyes and smiled.

"Why are you smiling?" LaTrell asked.

"Girl, it makes no sense how good Mr. Phillips smells," Shajuan said, shaking her head.

While Shajuan spoke, something caught LaTrell's eye. She adjusted her eyes to get a better look but wasn't sure what she was seeing.

Shajuan noticed LaTrell looking at her

strangely and smiled. "What are you looking at?" she asked.

"It looks like you have glitter on your nose," LaTrell said, squinting one eye.

Shajuan smiled. "That's my surprise," she said, as she came closer.

LaTrell's eyes grew wide. "You got your nose pierced?" she asked, inspecting Shajuan's nose like a doctor.

"No! It's not pierced. It's a stick-on nose stud. I got it when my dad came to visit during Halloween," Shajuan said, with a wide smile. "See, it's detachable." She took it off her right nostril and then put it back on again.

"Wow! Your dad let you get that? What did your mom say?" LaTrell asked, looking concerned.

"My dad doesn't care. He's the one who bought it for me." Shajuan paused for a second and continued, "And, um, my mama hasn't seen it yet. I take it off when I'm at home, so no one will catch me. My mom doesn't play. Since my dad doesn't see us that much, he pretty much lets us do what we want," Shajuan said, shrugging her shoulders.

Shajuan's new nose stud reminded LaTrell of Peaches from summer camp. Peaches did whatever she wanted; from hair dying to tattoos to wearing skimpy clothes, you name it, she did it.

And I can't even put a little color in my hair. This is so not fair. What can I try experimenting with, without my dad and Daryl finding out? LaTrell thought.

"Well, I should have known I would run into Ms. Tropical Island and Mouth from the South before lunch," Chandler said, making room for himself in the middle of them.

"Hey, Big Head," Shajuan said, trying to rub Chandler's head.

Chandler ducked as Shajuan reached for his head. "Hey! You have something shiny on your nose," Chandler said, motioning for Shajuan to brush her nose.

"It's a nose stud, genius," Shajuan said, rolling her eyes.

Chandler tilted his head to the side. "Shajuan Martinez! Are you crazy? Your nostrils are gonna turn green," he said, looking at Shajuan as if she had cooties.

"No they won't, silly," Shajuan said.

LaTrell and Shajuan giggled. All three of them had English class next, but with different teachers.

"All right, my peeps, I'll catch up with you at lunch," Chandler said, throwing up his signature two-finger peace sign.

"Okay!" LaTrell and Shajuan said at the same time.

LaTrell and Shajuan gave each other a high five and disappeared into their classrooms. As LaTrell made her way to her seat, she heard a voice say, "Hello there, LaTrell," with the letter *r* rolling off the tongue. LaTrell sat down and made eye contact with Mrs. Gassíon. LaTrell smiled and waved to her. Mrs. Gassíon was from Paris, France, and she had a heavy accent. LaTrell didn't mind that Mrs. Gassíon didn't pronounce her name correctly. Every day Mrs. Gassíon greeted each student by name as they walked into the classroom. She had curly red hair like the character Annie and an upbeat personality and voice like Mrs. Frizzle from the *Magic School Bus* show. She even wore different colors of eye shadow to match her outfits.

After staring at Ms. Gassíon for a few seconds, LaTrell had an idea. She remembered that Paulina's makeup was packed in the Precious Things box and that she could began trying out different shades of eye shadow to match her outfits, too. To keep it a secret, LaTrell would put on the makeup at school. LaTrell got excited as she replayed the idea over and over in her mind.

She came out of her thoughts at the sound of Ms. Gassíon clapping her hands three times. "This week you are going to work on a biography, which means you will write and provide details of life events. The last few months, you have worked on activities that focus on the five *w*'s. The five *w*'s are: *who, what, when, where,* and *why,*" Mrs. Gassíon said, in a delightful voice.

"Today you will select two inventors, one man and one woman. You will prepare a timeline of when their two or more inventions were created. Finally, prepare a biography, one to two pages long apiece, about each inventor, and include the five *w*'s," Mrs. Gassíon said, looking at each student. "By the way, this is also your homework. The projects are due next Monday. Let's get a move on."

When LaTrell got home from school, she was exhausted. Daryl had stayed after school to attend Boy Scouts, so she had the house to herself for a little while. LaTrell pulled the Precious Things box from underneath her bed and took out a handful of different eye shadows. She laid all of the makeup kits on the bed and opened each of them one by one to get a closer look. Each kit contained three different shades of one color. The dark shade was on the bottom, the medium shade was in the middle, and the lighter shade was on top.

LaTrell remembered watching the way Paulina had applied the eye shadow and filled in her eyebrows. LaTrell decided to replay the steps in her mind and practice with colors of the beige family. *I hope I do this right. I don't want to look like I belong in a circus act*, she said to herself. She leaned in closer to the mirror, lifted the sponge applicator out of the eye shadow kit, and applied the darker shade along the bottom of her right eyelid. Next, she applied the middle shade in the crease area, working from the outer corner of the eye. Finally, she applied the lightest shade in a windshield-wiper motion at the top of the eyelid and blended until the colors became softer. She repeated the same steps on her left eye.

When LaTrell finished, she turned her face from left to right to check out her work.

"Hmm . . . it doesn't look quite like how Mama did hers, but I don't think I did too bad," LaTrell said, smiling.

She plopped down on her bed, then slid to the floor and leaned over to get her journal out of the top drawer.

November 18
Hi Mama! Your baby girl is a little tired today. It looks like this year is going to be

filled with lots of projects. I think Dad is going to have to purchase a new computer and printer. Can you whisper to tell him where he needs to go to get a good deal? I sure hope he can buy one. Oh! Guess what! Shajuan got a stick-on nose stud. It's like our parents are opposite. Her dad seems to let her do what she wants and try new things, and her mother is the strict one. Just like Dad (smile). Mama, I know I'm only twelve years old, but do you think I'm too young to wear a little eye shadow? I put on some eye makeup, just like you used to. What do you think? How come the girls at school get to try out different things to make them look cool and I can't? Dad doesn't let me do much at all. Do you think he'll change his mind anytime soon? I sure hope so, Mama. Oh well, I need to go and warm up the leftovers and start on my homework. I'll try to write again before I go to bed. Love you, Mama!

LaTrell believed that if Paulina had been alive, LaTrell would have had a little more freedom to try new things. Paulina had a way of talking to Luis and getting him to keep an open mind, instead of just saying the word *no*. LaTrell hoped Luis would loosen up a bit. She didn't want to be looked at as the lame kid for not keeping up with the latest styles. Even though she polished nice designs on her fingernails and toenails, it wasn't cool enough for her.

LaTrell exhaled, making her top and bottom lip sound like a balloon losing air. She gathered up all of the eye shadow kits on her bed and hid them in her backpack. She placed her journal back in the drawer and got up to wash off her makeup. Luis and Daryl would be home soon, and she didn't want them to see her wearing eye shadow.

LaTrell put a casserole in the oven to warm up and sat at the kitchen table to begin her homework. The sound of keys jingled at the front door. Luis and Daryl were home.

"Oh boy! I can't wait to have some of that casserole again," Daryl said, licking his lips.

"Yeah, I bet you can't," Luis said, shaking his head and smiling.

"Hey there, Ms. LaTrell!" Luis said, bending down to give her a hug.

"Hi, Dad! I had a long day at school," LaTrell said.

"Well, what did you do?" Luis asked.

"In Technology, we were assigned to a computer to work on different tasks. In English, we have to research two inventors, create a timeline, and type up a biography on each one," LaTrell said.

"Oh, okay. That doesn't seem too bad," Luis said, while glancing over the mail.

"Well, since I must complete my English project as homework, I will need to work on a computer that's faster," LaTrell said slowly, while looking at Luis.

"What do you mean, a faster computer? Are you telling me the computer in there isn't good enough?" Luis asked, pointing toward the den, where the computer was located.

"Aww, Dad, I can squeeze honey out faster than the computer can load," Daryl said.

"Dad, I can barely read the words on the screen. Everything looks fuzzy. It started acting crazy when Mama worked on her last paper for school," LaTrell said.

"Hmm . . . I think I remember that," Luis said. Then he snapped his fingers and added, "I think I have a solution."

He went into the garage and came back carrying a funny-shaped object with a dusty black cover.

Luis unzipped the cover around to the other side and removed the item.

"What is that?" Daryl asked.

"Is that a typewriter?" LaTrell asked.

"Ding ding ding! You got it," Luis said, sounding proud.

LaTrell and Daryl sat in silence, looking at the typewriter.

"Why are you two looking like that? This is the real deal," Luis said, dusting it off.

"Why does it look funny?" Daryl asked.

"Dad, you can't do spell check on a typewriter," LaTrell said.

"And that's why we have two dictionaries and a thesaurus here," Luis said, as he continued cleaning off the typewriter.

"But, Dad, I can't do research on a typewriter or add clip art," LaTrell said, trying not to get upset.

"Clip who?" Luis asked.

"Dad, could you please consider buying a new computer and a printer?" LaTrell asked.

"We need a printer, too?" Luis asked.

"I can look for some sales in the newspaper," LaTrell said.

"I can help, too! That thing is scary," Daryl said, staring at the typewriter.

"Okay, okay. I'll look around to see what I can find. I guess I need to go ahead and schedule an appointment with Xfinity to upgrade to a faster Internet service while I'm at it," Luis said, looking at the kids, then at the typewriter.

Luis packed up the typewriter and took it back to the garage.

LaTrell let out a long sigh. "Boy, that was close," she said.

A few days later, two loud horn beeps sounded outside. Daryl stopped writing and looked at LaTrell. LaTrell dried her hands on a dish towel and came out of the kitchen. Daryl ran over to look out the window.

"It's Dad!" Daryl said, hurrying to open the front door.

LaTrell and Daryl met Luis at the car. Luis was bent over, looking into the trunk. "Hey there, kiddos. LaTrell, you grab the box from the backseat. Daryl, you close the trunk, and watch your fingers," Luis said, as he held up a big box.

Once they were inside the house, Luis and LaTrell placed the boxes on the table. Looking them over, Daryl asked, "Dad, what did you buy?"

"Best Buy had a computer-and-printer bundle

deal, so I decided to stop by after work to purchase it," Luis said, with a big smile.

LaTrell pulled the scissors out of the kitchen drawer and handed them to Luis. Luis carefully cut the boxes open and removed the computer monitor, hard drive, and printer.

"Ooh, this is cool, Dad!" Daryl said.

"Yeah, thank you, Dad," LaTrell said, leaning in to give Luis a side hug.

"I'm glad you guys like the computer. After dinner, I will set it up. It shouldn't take me long, since I have set up a few at work,"Luis said, as he moved the items to the computer desk.

As promised, Luis set up the computer. LaTrell and Daryl peered over his shoulder as he pushed the power button. They all expressed a sigh of relief when the computer screen lit up and functioned properly.

After cleaning the kitchen, LaTrell made sure she placed her book bag near the front door. Then she showered and got ready for bed. LaTrell tossed and turned and could not fall asleep. She was so excited about the new computer. *Well, since I can't go to sleep, I might as well try it out*, she decided. LaTrell got out of bed and slowly cracked her bedroom door. Luis's bedroom door was closed. Daryl snored so loudly, the neighbors probably heard him. Once

LaTrell determined everyone was asleep, she tiptoed out of her room and proceeded toward the den, where the computer was located. The only light reflected was the computer screen saver. She sat at the computer desk quietly. LaTrell moved the mouse until the icons on the desktop appeared. She clicked on the Internet Explorer icon. Next, LaTrell logged in to her school e-mail. There were two new message alerts. LaTrell clicked on the first message. It was a schoolwide e-mail about homecoming king and queen votes. She moved on to the next e-mail. The sender's name was alleyes_onme. The subject line read: *IT'S YOUR FAULT*.

LaTrell thought the name and subject line were odd, but she opened the e-mail anyway.

As her eyes moved from left to right, line by line, her mouth dropped.

The e-mail read: *I heard you are a motherless child and . . . ha ha . . .*

Underneath the text was a picture of a casket with a lightning bolt.

LaTrell quickly closed the e-mail and logged off. She rushed to her room as soon as she could, because she felt tears building up. LaTrell closed her bedroom door, plopped down on the bed, and stared at herself in the mirror in shock. Then she reached for the journal on the nightstand.

November 19

Mama, I'm so upset. Someone made fun of you dying. Why are people so cruel? What did I do to deserve this?

LaTrell tapped the pencil lightly on the paper as if she wanted to write more, but she couldn't. She was so hurt and felt violated. She closed the journal and placed it next to her. Lying down on her pillow, LaTrell wondered, *Who would write something like that?* Her tears fell one by one as she drifted off to sleep.

Chapter 4 Questions

1. Have you ever kept secrets from a family member or someone you were very close to?

2. Do you find yourself preferring the relative who says yes, the most?

3. No one likes to be told no. Can you recall a time when you were allowed to do something and later realized it didn't turn out the way you expected?

<u>Five</u>

Discovery

LaTrell dreaded getting out of bed. Her eyes felt like sandbags because she had lain awake most of the night. She grabbed the first pair of jeans and shirt within reach. She didn't care if they matched or needed ironing. Then she made her way to the kitchen and halfheartedly ate breakfast. She poked around in the cereal bowl as she replayed the e-mail over and over in her head.

"What's going on with you this morning?" Luis asked.

Startled by Luis's voice, LaTrell adjusted her sitting position and shrugged her shoulders.

"You might as well spit it out. I'm not going to send you to school with a long face," Luis said, standing over LaTrell.

"Yeah, long and ugly," Daryl said, as he smacked on his breakfast.

LaTrell rolled her eyes at Daryl.

"Nothing, Dad. I'm just tired. Daryl's snoring kept me up most of the night," LaTrell said, with a displeased look. She didn't want to tell Luis the truth.

Daryl stopped chewing his food and said, "Uh-uh, that wasn't me. I don't snore."

Luis and LaTrell both looked at Daryl and said, "Oh, yes, you do!"

Daryl thought about it for a few minutes. "Ha ha, you two got jokes," he said, and resumed eating.

Soon after that, LaTrell and Daryl collected their things and headed to school. LaTrell couldn't wait to show Shajuan the rude e-mail during computer class. As luck would have it, Mr. Phillips was absent and there was a substitute in his place. Even though the substitute followed Mr. Phillips's directions aloud, some of the students did their own thing, like sitting with friends and not staying in their seat.

LaTrell motioned for Shajuan to come sit next to her.

"Hey, girl!" Shajuan said, taking a seat next to LaTrell.

"Hi," LaTrell said, giving Shajuan a strange look.

"What's wrong with you?" Shajuan asked.

LaTrell took a deep breath. "You're not going to believe this."

"What?" Shajuan asked.

"My dad bought a new computer for the house yesterday. I was so excited that I couldn't sleep. When everyone was asleep, I snuck out of my room to get on the computer. I logged on to the school e-mail and saw this," LaTrell said, as she used the mouse to maximize a window on the computer.

Shajuan turned her head to look at the monitor. LaTrell watched Shajuan's face as she read the e-mail. Shajuan's mouth dropped open.

"LaTrell! What in the world? Who sent this? Do you think it was from someone in this class?" Shajuan asked, looking angrily around the classroom.

"I don't know. The sender's name was alleyes_onme, from a Yahoo! account. The school e-mail should only include the first name, last name, and school name," LaTrell said, pointing at the screen. "We weren't allowed to make up nicknames, remember?" Then, in a softer voice, she said, "I haven't told my dad yet. What do you think I should do?"

"Oh, LaTrell, I don't know what to say. This is beyond rude," Shajuan said, shaking her head and thinking about how she was still keeping her clip-on nose ring a secret from her mother. "What do you want to do?" Shajuan asked.

"Honestly? I would like to punch the person who said these words in the mouth. But since I don't know who it is yet, I'll just fight back with words."

"Wow! As long as we've been friends, I've never seen you so upset that you want to hit someone. I'm usually the one who fights first and talks later," Shajuan said.

LaTrell looked at Shajuan, not knowing what to say next.

"Whatever you decide, I got your back," Shajuan said.

LaTrell turned her attention back to the computer. She clicked the REPLY button at the top of the e-mail and typed, *I bet you won't say those words to my FACE!!!!!* Mr. Phillips had told the class that writing in all caps would let the reader know that you were shouting.

"How does this sound?" LaTrell asked.

"Sounds good to me," Shajuan said.

LaTrell clicked the SEND button and hoped to get a response.

During lunch that day, LaTrell and Shajuan told Chandler about the e-mail and how LaTrell had responded to it.

"Oh, snap! Now that's low-down," Chandler said in disbelief.

"Yeah, that's what I said. That e-mail has my best friend ready to fight, too," Shajuan said, squeezing LaTrell's shoulders.

Chandler looked at LaTrell with a puzzled expression and said, "LaTrell, fighting? No way. You are way too prissy. You go crazy when one of your fingernails chips. I know you can't take a punch."

"First of all, what makes you think I would stand there long enough to get hit?" LaTrell said.

"I guess she told you," Shajuan said, snapping her fingers in the shape of the letter *Z*.

"Whoa, don't beat me up. I'm just saying, you're usually the calm one. Shajuan is the beat-'em-up machine," Chandler said, pointing at Shajuan.

"You don't think I can defend myself?" LaTrell asked.

"I didn't say you couldn't. I've never seen you fight or even argue with anyone. That's all," Chandler said.

"Well, how would you feel if someone said that about one of your parents?" LaTrell asked.

"I can't lie. I might react the same way," Chandler said.

"Well, you already know what I would do," Shajuan said, making an *I wish you would* face.

"Yes, we do," LaTrell and Chandler said at the same time, laughing.

"Ooh, wait a minute—this situation reminds me of my fifteen-year-old cousin, Lisa," Shajuan said. "Have you guys heard of Instagram?" she asked.

LaTrell and Chandler both shook their heads yes.

Shajuan popped the bubblegum she was chewing, before she continued talking. "Well, last year my cousin Lisa used Instagram to communicate with her friends from school and show off her fashion style. Some girls she knew through a mutual friend begin to follow her page. Next thing you know, these girls started posting mean things about her for everyone to see and sent her private threatening messages, too. Things got pretty ugly," Shajuan said, slowly lowering her voice.

"What happened to your cousin?" LaTrell asked.

"Yeah, what happened?" Chandler asked, slurping his juice through a small straw.

"Lisa told her mother, my Aunt Celia. And then my aunt reported the girls to the police and made Lisa shut down her Instagram page," Shajuan said.

"The police?" LaTrell said, sounding shocked.

"Yep, Lisa said she will never get on social media again. It's been a whole year now, and she still hasn't done so. Since this happened to Lisa, my mama won't let me set up an Instagram page. She's too nervous. Plus, she says she's too old to be fighting anyone these days," Shajuan said.

"I see the apple doesn't fall too far from the tree," Chandler said, looking at Shajuan.

Sometimes LaTrell felt like she missed out on having things, like a social media page and a cell phone. Luis and Paulina had agreed to wait until LaTrell and Daryl each turned thirteen before they were permitted to have these things.

"I think we should put our detective skills to work and find out who this alleyes_onme person is," Shajuan said.

LaTrell and Chandler nodded in agreement.

"Okay, this is the plan," Shajuan said, as LaTrell and Chandler leaned in closer.

"While LaTrell waits for a response, we need to listen more closely to the conversations that take place in the classroom," Shajuan said.

LaTrell and Chandler agreed.

"Oh, and LaTrell, you need to be more aware of how people look at you," Shajuan said.

"What do you mean?" LaTrell asked.

"What I mean is, you need to pay attention to see if people look at you funny or stare at you longer than usual," Shajuan said, pointing at her eyes with her index finger.

"Yep!" Chandler said, licking Dorito crumbs off his fingers.

"Oh," LaTrell said softly.

Shajuan and Chandler did most of the talking, as if they had both experienced this before. Oddly enough, LaTrell wasn't scared. She just wanted to know who had sent that e-mail, and why.

After lunch, all three of them headed toward their classes. Chandler and Shajuan were busy chatting about the e-mail and what they would do if they were in LaTrell's shoes. LaTrell zoned out of the conversation and looked at students as they crossed her path and passed by her. She followed Shajuan's instructions. LaTrell would continue with this paranoid behavior until she found out who was behind the e-mail. Unfortunately, LaTrell had no idea what she was getting herself into.

November 20
Hi Mama, I'm still upset. I just feel like fighting, Mama. I just feel like fighting. I've never felt this angry before. Wouldn't you want to fight if someone said this to you about Adela? Why don't I get the feeling that you agree with me?

LaTrell had been writing to Paulina long enough that she developed a spiritual connection and knew when her presence could be felt. She could sense when Paulina smiled. This was one of those times when LaTrell knew Paulina wasn't smiling.

***

Throughout the week, LaTrell anxiously checked her school e-mail every day, hoping to see a reply from the unknown sender, but there was no response. Chandler and Shajuan checked in on a regular basis for updates, like two investigators.

"Nothing so far, guys," LaTrell would say.

The Saturday before Thanksgiving, after completing her chores, LaTrell plopped down in the recliner and exhaled. She had the house to herself because Luis and Daryl had gone to the barbershop to get haircuts. Enjoying the peace and quiet for a few minutes, LaTrell decided to log on and check her school e-mail.

The e-mail home page showed five new messages. At that moment, LaTrell's heart began to beat quickly. She scrolled down the page slowly until she came to the first unread e-mail. The subject line read: *Message from Principal Willingham.*

LaTrell didn't bother to read it, since his e-mails were always superlong motivational speeches.

She moved down to the next e-mail, titled *Hey Girl!*

LaTrell opened the e-mail and saw that Shajuan had sent her a test message. LaTrell chuckled after reading it.

"That girl is so crazy," LaTrell said, as she laughed out loud.

So far, so good, she said to herself. She continued on to the third message. It was a school-wide IT maintenance alert.

"They're always running tests," LaTrell said, shaking her head.

She moved on to the next e-mail, titled *What's poppin'?* The message read: *What's up, LaTrell? This is your boy Chandler the Man. Respond back to me so I know if you got this e-mail or not. Peace!*

LaTrell smiled and thought, *Who in the world told Chandler that he was a man?*

LaTrell clicked the REPLY button and typed, *Hey, Chandler the Boy! You are funny*. Then she clicked the SEND button.

LaTrell started to feel at ease, until she read the subject line of the last e-mail: *Think U R tough?*

LaTrell gripped the mouse tightly as her index

finger left-clicked on the message.

The message read: *If your face wasn't so ugly, I wouldn't have a problem saying anything to your face. M-o-t-h-e-r-l-e-s-s c-h-i-l-d!! Ha ha ha.*

A blank stare came over LaTrell's face. Then it deepened into a scowl.

Hmph! So you think I'm ugly, huh? LaTrell thought, as she positioned her fingers on the keyboard.

She glanced up at the computer screen, and the fear that had taken over her the first time she had seen the message turned into something else. With a mischievous smile, she typed the word *COWARD!!!* on the subject line. In the message box, LaTrell went on to write, *You sure do talk a lot of junk! You keep messing with me, and my mama just might pay you a visit for being mean to her daughter. Are you ready for that visit? Ha ha, scaredy-cat.*

LaTrell sat back in the chair to reread her message before pressing the SEND button. When the message disappeared, LaTrell found herself in a weird place that she couldn't explain. She still wasn't scared, but there was a mixture of emotions she felt each time she received and replied to those e-mails.

The week of Thanksgiving, the e-mail

exchange between LaTrell and the cyber-bully continued. It was difficult enough getting used to not having Paulina around during that time. The last thing LaTrell wanted was to be insulted and not defend herself. The e-mails increased in frequency from once a week to two and three times a week. Without any reason, LaTrell chose not to inform Chandler and Shajuan about most of those messages. She revealed only what a few of the e-mails said and brushed it off like they were no big deal, but deep down inside she was hurting and had grown tired of the rudeness and insults. Still, she wasn't ready to back down.

LaTrell's behavior changed drastically, and she wasn't her normal upbeat self. She became moody, developed a smart mouth with Luis when he tried to talk to her, and snapped at Daryl whenever he asked questions. Luis and Darryl knew something was going on, though they had no idea what it was. The dinner table was usually the central meeting place in the evenings where everyone reported how their day had gone, discussed the latest happenings in the neighborhood, and shared any other family news. Since the cyber-bullying issues had begun, LaTrell put only a small amount of food on her plate so she could finish eating more quickly, to avoid participating in conversation or answering questions. Not really paying attention, Luis assumed LaTrell ate fast because she was going through a growth spurt. Daryl wasn't putting too much thought into LaTrell's behavior. He was just being Daryl.

December 1
Hi Mama! I've been dealing with a lot of drama these last few weeks! Did you miss me? Goodness, I don't know where to start. Remember the last time I told you that someone sent me a mean e-mail? Well, they haven't stopped. In fact, they've gotten worse. I don't like the way I'm feeling or acting. I don't even have an appetite. I haven't told any adult besides you. Do you think I should tell Dad?

In the back of LaTrell's mind, she already knew the answer. However, she still wanted to handle it in her own way. LaTrell shut the journal and rushed into the kitchen to find something quick to eat. It was the first week back after the Thanksgiving holiday.

Daryl had just finished up his breakfast. He walked to the sink to rinse out his cereal bowl. While doing so, Daryl looked over at LaTrell and saw that her jeans were hanging off her waist. His eyes continued to move up like an elevator and stopped when he noticed LaTrell's eyes. He observed the redness in the corners and the slight puffiness underneath them.

Daryl cut the water off, put his bowl and spoon in the dish rack, and dried his hands. Then he said, "Hey, LaTrell, I think you're missing something."

LaTrell finished closing a box of muffins and gave Daryl a confused look. "Like what?" she asked.

"Like a belt," Daryl said, pointing at her jeans.

LaTrell followed Daryl's finger and looked down at her jeans. She felt her face flush. She wished she could disappear inside a shell, like a turtle. She had been so caught up in her own world that she hadn't noticed she was losing weight. But when she realized Daryl was waiting on a response, she quickly straightened her face.

"Oh! I knew that. I just wanted to hurry up and find something to eat for breakfast before it's time to leave," LaTrell said nonchalantly, while adjusting her jeans and folding the top section over.

"Did you also know that you're still wearing your head scarf, too?" Daryl asked, looking at the top of LaTrell's head.

LaTrell lifted her right hand to touch her head and gave Daryl the side-eye.

"Yes, Daryl. I want to make sure my edges lie smooth, since I'm wearing a ponytail. Why are you paying so much attention to me, anyway?" LaTrell asked.

"I always pay attention to you, even when you think I'm not. You've been acting a little weird lately. What's the matter?" Daryl asked.

"Whatever, Daryl. I think you're imagining things. There's nothing wrong with me," LaTrell said, waving him off.

"You know God thinks I'm the special one in this family. He blessed me with the gift of reading minds," Daryl said, trying to gaze into LaTrell's eyes.

"Oh, really? Well, what am I thinking now?" LaTrell asked, placing her right hand on her hip and smirking at him.

"I'll leave you alone for now," Daryl said, holding both hands up in the air. "Just know your big brother is watching you," he added, giving LaTrell a strange look.

"You mean little brother," LaTrell said, shaking her head.

Although Daryl was three years younger than LaTrell, he was wise beyond his years and generally operated as a big brother—or so he thought.

LaTrell unwrapped her muffin and took a bite. As she chewed, all kinds of thoughts crowded her mind. *When did I lose weight? Why am I forgetting stuff? Am I going crazy?* LaTrell now recognized that she wasn't doing a good job of hiding her feelings after all. She wondered, if Daryl was paying attention to her, who else was.

LaTrell looked at the clock, took another bite of her muffin, and threw it in the garbage. It was time to go. She quickly went back to her bedroom to look herself over in the mirror. LaTrell made sure she put on a belt, removed her head scarf, and put on a light, waist-length sweater to camouflage the slight bagginess in her jeans.

***

That morning in the hallway, LaTrell, Chandler, and Shajuan stood in front of their lockers, talking as they usually did before the first bell rang.

"I don't know about y'all, but I haven't heard anyone talking about sending prank e-mails," Chandler said, looking at LaTrell, then Shajuan.

"Me either," Shajuan said.

LaTrell shook her head and said, "Neither have I."

She couldn't bear to tell them about the last e-mail she had received before Thanksgiving.

"I almost forgot," Chandler said. He reached inside his book bag and pulled out a thin, shiny, folded piece of paper.

"What's that?" Shajuan asked.

"This weekend I went to Urgent Care with my grandma. Since it was so boring in the waiting room, I opened one of those PBS Kids magazines," Chandler said, tapping his index finger on his right temple.

LaTrell and Shajuan looked at each other and back at Chandler.

"When I turned a few pages, this title, in bold red letters, jumped out at me like a police siren," Chandler said, as he unfolded the paper.

LaTrell and Shajuan chuckled.

"No, I'm serious. Look!" Chandler said, holding the torn-out magazine page in front of the girls.

The title, "Stand Up to Cyber-bullying," stood out, just like Chandler had said.

LaTrell slid the paper from Chandler's hands and leaned in a little closer to read the small print. As she read, Chandler gave an overview of the article. Anytime he explained or presented information, he looked like a teacher, because he loved to use his hands.

"Did you know cyber-bullying is very common in middle school–age kids (eleven to thirteen)?" Without waiting for anyone to answer the question, he continued, "The article said at least 52 percent of teens do not report cyber-bullying to their parents." He paused and looked at LaTrell. "But the worst part of all is that some kids have committed suicide because of this," Chandler said, tapping LaTrell's shoulder with his index and middle fingers.

LaTrell looked up from the paper. Her eyes met Chandler's eyes.

"Are you sure you don't want to tell your dad, LaTrell?" Chandler asked.

"How long are you going to wait?" Shajuan asked.

LaTrell looked down at the ground, then at Chandler and Shajuan.

"I don't know," she said in a low voice.

"LaTrell, I'm beginning to think you're not taking this seriously," Chandler said.

"Mm-hmm, lately you've been acting like you don't have a care in the world, or like it's no big deal. You know I'm not one to back down from a fight. But that doesn't mean I don't get scared," Shajuan said, looking at LaTrell.

"LaTrell, what are you waiting on? You need to tell your dad and report this to Mr. Phillips," Chandler said, with both hands extended wide.

"Well, how do you all expect me to act? Who made you two the boss of me?" LaTrell asked. She felt herself getting upset. "I'm handling this the best way I can. I'm not perfect. No one is making fun of your parents. Since you two think I'm not good enough for you, just leave me alone," LaTrell said, rolling her eyes as she passed in between them.

Chandler's mouth dropped, and Shajuan gasped. They both watched LaTrell disappear down the hallway.

"LaTrell is *h-o-t* with us," Shajuan said, spelling out the word *hot*. "I think our friend may be in denial. What are we going to do?" she asked, looking helplessly at Chandler.

Chandler shook his head and shrugged his shoulders. Surprisingly, he found himself speechless. LaTrell had never spoken to them like that before. The girl he had known since kindergarten suddenly felt like a stranger.

***

LaTrell felt tears forming in the corners of her eyes. She didn't want anyone to see her upset, so she went inside the girls' bathroom. Just as LaTrell closed and locked the stall door, the tears rushed down her face like raindrops against a window. *Why is this happening to me?* she wondered. She hadn't cried like this since the day Paulina died. Her breathing got heavier and heavier, until she felt dizzy. LaTrell rested her body against the stall door and slid down little by little. She felt like her chest was vibrating to a bass drum.

"Mama, please help me!" LaTrell said in a low, trembling voice with her eyes closed.

Shhh . . . It's okay, I'm watching, a voice said faintly. LaTrell's eyes popped open, and she looked from left to right as she took a deep breath. LaTrell knew Paulina was with her.

After she took another few deep breaths, the loud thumping in her chest went away and her tears stopped flowing. LaTrell stood still for a few seconds, waiting to hear Paulina's whisper again, but a few noisy students burst into the restroom and startled her. LaTrell straightened her clothes and gathered her belongings. After she heard the other stall doors close, she quickly went to the sink to flush her eyes with cold water. LaTrell leaned in to look at herself in the mirror. Her eyes were so swollen, they looked like they were in 3-D. She patted them again with a wet paper towel and exited the bathroom.

LaTrell entered the computer class and saw that a few students were already seated. She saw Shajuan out of the corner of her eye but didn't look her way. Instead, LaTrell sat down and took her notebook from her bookbag. When she looked up, Mr. Phillips was standing in front of her.

"Good morning, LaTrell. Are you okay?" Mr. Phillips asked.

"Yes, sir. I must have had an allergic reaction to something I ate for breakfast. But I'm okay," LaTrell said unconvincingly.

"Ah, I see. I hope the swelling goes down as the day continues. If it gets any worse, make sure you stop by the clinic to see the nurse," Mr. Phillips said, patting LaTrell on the shoulder.

Shajuan overheard Mr. Phillips and LaTrell's conversation. She knew LaTrell had been crying and wasn't telling the truth. Shajuan wanted so badly to go over and check on LaTrell, but she knew LaTrell was still upset with her. *My friend needs help. How can I help her?* Shajuan thought.

***

As the day went on, LaTrell felt the swelling in her eyes subside. She had calmed down by lunchtime, but instead of going inside the cafeteria, LaTrell went to the library instead. She wasn't hungry and wanted to be by herself. Besides, the library was quiet enough to allow her to get her thoughts together.

LaTrell took a seat at one of the tables in the back. She felt a headache coming on and started massaging her temples.

"Mama, please finish whispering to me. I need you to help me through this," LaTrell said with her eyes closed.

And just like that, she felt a sense of calmness being poured over her body like glaze being poured over a doughnut. LaTrell opened her eyes. She knew exactly what that meant. It was time to inform Luis about the cyber-bully.

***

Later that day at home, LaTrell replayed the different events that she had experienced recently, from the cyber-bully's e-mails to the article Chandler had shared to the weight loss that Daryl had pointed out to her. *Do kids actually kill themselves because of what someone has said or done to them?* LaTrell wondered.

She lay on top of her comforter, curled up, and dozed off. Taking a nap after school had become the norm for her these last few months. She had driven herself crazy trying to handle the bully situation and keep it a secret.

When the smell of food seeped under LaTrell's door, she immediately sat up. *Oh no! I'm supposed to be warming up dinner*, she remembered. She hurriedly went to the bathroom to wash her face. When LaTrell walked out of the bathroom, she met Luis coming around the corner.

"Hey there, sleeping beauty!" he said, smiling, but his smile quickly turned into a worried look. "Are you feeling okay? Your eyes look heavy," Luis asked.

"Yes, I'm fine. I've just been more tired lately," LaTrell said.

"Whose shorts are you wearing? Why do you have the top of the shorts folded over twice?" Luis asked, looking LaTrell up and down.

"Aunt Roberta brought these for me a while back. She picked up the wrong size, but I still wanted to keep them because they're comfortable," LaTrell said, as she began walking past Luis.

Luis placed his hand on LaTrell's shoulder to prevent her from taking another step.

"LaTrell, who do you think you're fooling? I wasn't born yesterday. What's going on?" Luis asked.

LaTrell took a deep breath, and her eyes begin to fill up with tears. "Dad, I need to show you something," she said, walking toward the den.

"What is it? Did you or Daryl break something?" Luis asked, as he walked behind her.

LaTrell turned her head slightly to look back at Luis, but she didn't answer him. She approached the computer desk and sat down.

"Oh no! Don't tell me the computer is broken already," Luis exclaimed.

"There's nothing wrong with the computer," LaTrell said, trying to sound convincing. "Remember the night that you set up the computer? Well, I couldn't sleep, so I decided to check my school e-mail and I saw this," LaTrell said, pointing at the screen.

Luis bent down to view the content more closely. After he finished reading, he slowly stood up straight. LaTrell looked up at him.

"Baby girl, I'm so sorry. This is just flat-out mean and uncalled for. Do you know who sent this?" Luis asked, shaking his head.

"No, but the sender's name is alleyes_onme, and it's from a Yahoo! account," LaTrell said.

"LaTrell, you've been keeping this a secret all this time?" Luis asked.

LaTrell nodded her head yes.

"I'm going to get to the bottom of this and see the principal tomorrow morning," Luis said, sounding upset.

The next morning, Luis and LaTrell arrived at school and walked into the principal's office. LaTrell took a seat on one of the benches while Luis stood at the counter to speak with the secretary.

"Mr. Willingham will be right out," said the secretary.

"Thank you," Luis said, as he took a seat.

LaTrell watched teachers come into and out of the office to sign in and check their mailboxes. A loud group of students and two adults burst into the office, yelling at one another and arguing. Apparently, the students had misbehaved on the bus and gotten in trouble with the bus driver.

LaTrell was so caught up in the commotion that she didn't notice Mr. Phillips speaking to her at first, but then Luis nudged LaTrell with his elbow and motioned for her to turn toward her right.

"Oh, good morning, Mr. Phillips!" LaTrell said.

"Good morning to you. I was beginning to think you were ignoring me," Mr. Phillips said, smiling.

"I didn't hear you with all of this noise," LaTrell said, pointing to the group in front of them.

"Yeah, I see. I can barely hear myself," Mr. Phillips said.

"How are you doing? I'm LaTrell's father. It's nice to meet you," Luis said, extending his hand.

"Yes, sir. I'm well. I'm Mr. Phillips, LaTrell's Technology teacher," he said, as he shook Luis's hand. "Is everything okay?" Mr. Phillips asked.

LaTrell and Luis looked at each other.

"Well, we have a little situation here. LaTrell showed me a very mean e-mail she received yesterday, and—"

Luis was about to explain the problem, when a deep voice interrupted. "Good morning, Mr. Wiggins. I'm sorry to keep you waiting. How may I help you?" Mr. Willingham asked, standing at the office counter.

"Hi, Principal Willingham. I was just about to explain the issue to Mr. Phillips. Do you mind if he joins us?" Luis asked.

"I don't mind at all. Let's take a seat here in my conference area." Mr. Willingham pointed and led the way.

Once they were inside the room, everyone gathered around a large oval table and sat in oversize orange chairs with wheels. The walls were covered with charts, graphs, and targets for an upcoming school-wide test.

"Thank you for your time this morning. I'm here because my daughter, LaTrell, showed me a very disturbing e-mail. You see, my wife, Paulina, passed away a little over a year ago. It's been a little rough at times, but for the most part we're adjusting," Luis said, looking over at LaTrell.

"I'm sorry for your loss," Mr. Willingham said.

"So am I," Mr. Phillips said next.

"Thank you," Luis said. "Apparently, another student is aware of this and is poking fun at the fact that LaTrell lost her mother," Luis added, biting his lip.

"What?" Mr. Phillips said, shocked.

"Was this e-mail sent using the school's e-mail? Or was this a personal one?" Mr. Willingham asked.

"It was a personal e-mail sent to my school e-mail," LaTrell said.

Mr. Phillips reached into his backpack and pulled out his laptop. "LaTrell, I'm going to turn on my laptop. I would like for you to log on to your school e-mail," Mr. Phillips said, as he sat the laptop on the table.

"Good idea," Mr. Willingham said.

LaTrell entered her information. She opened

the e-mail and turned the laptop toward Principal Willingham and Mr. Phillips.

Mr. Phillips's eyes grew wide as he scrolled down the page. Principal Willingham's face turned red. Both men looked at each other and then at Luis and LaTrell.

"LaTrell, these e-mails date all the way back to November 19. Why didn't you report this when it first happened?" Principal Willingham asked.

LaTrell shrugged her shoulders. She was too ashamed to say that she had wanted to handle the situation her way.

"I also see that you replied to a lot of these e-mails. Usually, retaliation significantly complicates matters. LaTrell, this could have gotten a lot worse," Mr. Phillips said, looking up from the e-mails and at LaTrell.

LaTrell looked down at the table. She knew she had let this go on far too long.

With a serious look, Principal Willingham said, "Mr. Wiggins and LaTrell, let me be the first to apologize for this cruel and senseless act. I do not encourage, nor will I stand for, this type of behavior. I will make it my top priority to find out who sent this e-mail and deal with them accordingly."

"That's what I wanted to hear. This individual

needs to know that words do hurt. I know it may not be easy to find the person behind this, but if you do, I would like for him or her to apologize to my daughter," Luis said, putting his hand on LaTrell's shoulder.

"You bet an apology will be in order, among other things," Mr. Willingham said, looking at Mr. Phillips.

"I'm so sorry this happened. When we originally thought of issuing school e-mails to students, we wanted to put all sorts of security measures in place to protect them," Mr. Phillips said.

"We also thought our system would block any personal e-mails from getting through. Somewhere along the way, we failed and need to find the loopholes," Principal Willingham said.

"I guess I need to put on my tech hat and trace who this e-mail belongs to," Mr. Phillips said.

"I will also report this incident to our school resource officer. He will help investigate this as well," Principal Willingham said.

The first bell rang, and everyone stood up.

"Thanks again for your time," Mr. Wiggins said.

"It was my pleasure. Don't hesitate to bring any more problems to me. It is my job to ensure my students' safety," Principal Willingham said, as he shook Luis's hand again and nodded at LaTrell.

LaTrell and Luis walked out of the office, followed by Principal Willingham and Mr. Phillips.

"Okay, sweetie, I must get to work now. I'll see you at home later this evening," Luis said, as he gave LaTrell a hug.

"Bye, Dad," LaTrell said.

***

Chandler grabbed LaTrell's shoulder from behind as she walked toward homeroom. "LaTrell, when was the last time you had your hearing checked?" he asked.

LaTrell gave Chandler a weird look. "What do you mean?"

"Girl, I called your name three times in my deepest voice, and you didn't turn around once," Chandler said, looking concerned.

"Oh! I guess I have a lot on my mind and wasn't paying attention," LaTrell said.

"Yeah, you've been very snappy lately. I saw your dad leave. Is there anything you want to tell Counselor Chandler?"

"I finally told my dad about the cyber-bully," LaTrell said, with a sigh of relief. "We just had a meeting with Principal Willingham and Mr. Phillips."

"Well, let the church say, 'Amen!'" Chandler said, raising both of his hands high.

LaTrell burst out laughing—something she had not done in a long time.

"You had me and Shajuan worried," Chandler said.

LaTrell looked at Chandler and said, "I'm sorry for the way I snapped at you."

"So, does this mean you and I are back on good terms now?" Chandler asked.

LaTrell shook her head yes.

"Good! 'Cause no one can go without a little bit of Chandler in their life for too long," Chandler said sarcastically.

"Bye, Chandler. Go to class," LaTrell said, rolling her eyes to the ceiling, softly pushing him to the left.

They both continued in opposite directions to their classes. LaTrell felt uneasy as she approached Technology. She opened the door and sat down at her computer. She could hear a group of students snickering in the back of the room. LaTrell noticed a few students on the right-side staring at her. On the left side, a few students pointed at her and whispered.

Why are they looking at me? LaTrell wondered.

Then a voice from the back of the room said, "Hey, LaTrell, are you really a motherless child?"

A few giggles erupted all over the classroom.

LaTrell gasped. She recognized Kevin's voice. They had attended the same school since the first grade. "What did you say?" she asked, as she turned around slowly, squinting. "Why would you make fun of my mother dying?" she said, through clenched teeth.

LaTrell's heart pounded very fast as she felt a rush of anxiety from her head to her toes. Both of her hands were balled up in tight fists. She got up from her seat and walked toward the boy who had said those words. As LaTrell got closer, a hush fell over the room.

"So, *you're* the one who's been sending those mean e-mails to me? What's so funny about my mama dying of cancer? Do you know how much pain she was in? I guess you have never lost anyone. And what have I ever done to you?" LaTrell said, with tears streaming down her face. "I should knock you out of that chair," she added, raising her right fist.

"No, girl! Don't do it. He's not worth it," Shajuan said, stepping in between LaTrell and Kevin.

"What's going on here?" Mr. Phillips asked, blowing his whistle. He had been across the hall, assisting a substitute teacher.

"Kevin is the one who sent me those horrible e-mails," LaTrell said, as her tears continued to flow.

"I sent the e-mails, but I didn't write those words," Kevin said.

"Well, who did?" Mr. Phillips asked.

"My cousin who's in high school said those things," Kevin answered.

"Kevin, one of the rules of our acceptable-use policy states, 'Users of technological resources may not send electronic communications fraudulently (i.e., by misrepresenting the identity of the sender).' You clearly violated this rule, and you will have to face some consequences," Mr. Phillips said in a firm voice.

Kevin's smirk turned into a blank stare, then a look of regret, as he looked from Mr. Phillips to LaTrell and down at the floor.

Mr. Phillips walked over to push the red button on the wall. "Front office!" the secretary from the office answered. "Front office!"

Shajuan led LaTrell back to her seat. She was still upset. Another student got the Kleenex box off Mr. Phillips's desk and gave it to LaTrell.

"Yes, can you send Mr. Willingham to my

room, please? I have a situation," Mr. Phillips stated.

The room fell silent.

Mr. Willingham came into the room as if he were doing his morning power walk. "What's the problem here?" he asked.

Mr. Phillips pulled Mr. Willingham to the corner and began to whisper. While Mr. Phillips explained the issue, Mr. Willingham looked over the rims of his glasses at Kevin, then at LaTrell, and then back at Kevin. After Mr. Phillips finished explaining what had happened, Mr. Willingham walked over to LaTrell. "Are you okay?" he asked.

LaTrell nodded her head yes while she blew her nose.

"Young man, get your things and come with me," Mr. Willingham said. "LaTrell, after you pick up your lunch, I want you to go to the counselor's office. Mrs. Everett will be waiting for you."

LaTrell whispered, "Okay."

When the door closed behind them, the students began to talk among themselves about what had just taken place. The classroom became loud all over again.

"All right, all right—quiet down," Mr. Phillips said. Once the room was silent, he continued, "I need everybody's attention. What you just witnessed is a prime example of why it is important to follow rules. When you don't, you risk hurting others or yourself. There is no humor in losing a loved one. For those of you who thought it was funny, shame on you. Take a moment and put yourself in LaTrell's shoes. How would you feel? My point is, think before you act," Mr. Phillips said, looking from left to right. "You have about thirty minutes left in class. Get back to work." He turned and walked toward his desk.

Before the class ended, LaTrell received several hand-written notes from the students in the class, saying they were sorry. She read each one of them and then placed them inside her book bag.

As the day went on, LaTrell wondered if she would have to deal with any more mean students like Kevin. She hoped never to experience anything like this again. She couldn't help but think about Kevin. She had always known him to be a mild-mannered boy, not mean-spirited. He was the baby of three kids and lived in a house with his mom, aunt, and cousins. Kevin's mom worked two full-time jobs and never had time to attend any school activities. LaTrell remembered a field trip they had taken back in the third grade, to the High Museum. Almost every student's parent had attended, except a few. Kevin was one of them. He had seemed sad, so Paulina had invited him to join her and LaTrell's group. She had even treated him to a small souvenir. Kevin had been grateful and had given Paulina a hug. *Why would Kevin do this to me?* LaTrell thought to herself.

By the time lunch rolled around, LaTrell was starving. She remembered that she hadn't eaten breakfast that morning. While standing in the lunch line, LaTrell looked over at Shajuan and said, "I'm sorry I got an attitude with you earlier."

"It's okay. I realize now you were under a lot of pressure," Shajuan said, arranging the food items on her plate. "I just want to see my friend happy again," she added, nudging LaTrell with a smile.

LaTrell cracked half a smile in return. She and Shajuan grabbed their trays, and LaTrell headed toward the exit to go to the counselor's office. Just as she was about to walk out the door, Chandler came in. "Hey! Where are you going?" he asked, with his book bag hanging off his shoulder.

"To the counselor's office," LaTrell said.

Chandler focused on LaTrell's face. He could tell she had been crying. "All right, then I'll catch up with you after school," he said, looking concerned.

LaTrell began walking again, and Chandler turned back to look at her. Then he poked Shajuan's arm and asked, "Hey, what's up with LaTrell?"

"I'll tell you as soon as we sit down to eat," Shajuan said.

LaTrell cautiously walked the halls to avoid having her tray knocked over by the rowdy sixth-graders who thought it was okay to race in the hallway. She approached Mrs. Everett's office, where the door was propped open, and stopped. Mrs. Everett was on the phone. She looked up to see LaTrell and motioned for her to come in. LaTrell walked in and sat down at a big, round table located in the middle. Mrs. Everett finished her conversation and hung up the phone. She got up from her desk and walked over to LaTrell.

"Hi, LaTrell. I'm Mrs. Everett, the seventh-grade counselor. It's nice to meet you," she said, extending her hand and smiling widely.

"It's nice to meet you, too," LaTrell said, shaking Mrs. Everett's hand.

"Go ahead and eat your lunch while it's still warm. I'm going to grab my lunch bag as well and join you. Is that okay?" Mrs. Everett asked.

"Yes, ma'am," LaTrell replied in a soft voice.

LaTrell took her fork out of the package and ate

her spaghetti. Mrs. Everett placed her big pink lunch bag on the table and took items out one by one.

"Principal Willingham informed me this morning about the cyber-bullying issue you experienced and thought it would be a good idea for you to talk with someone. What kinds of thoughts ran through your mind after you read those e-mails?" Mrs. Everett asked.

LaTrell finished chewing her food and spoke. "At first, I didn't know what to think. I kept picturing those images of the casket and lightning bolt over and over, so much that I became sad all over again. This is my first time being teased about my mom's death. Why are people so cruel?" LaTrell asked, with a troubled look.

Mrs. Everett shook her head, as if she was disappointed. "It can happen for a number of reasons. The person can be hurting deep inside and want others to feel his or her pain. Or the individual might think they are being funny but not really know the extent of the consequences that may come with their actions," Mrs. Everett said.

LaTrell leaned in, placed her left elbow on the table, and propped her head in her left hand. She wondered if Kevin was sad or mad about his mom never being involved at school. Despite what had happened, she felt sorry for him.

LaTrell felt comfortable with Mrs. Everett. Her voice was smooth, like that of an evening-radio personality. She spoke in a way that was easy to understand and provided answers to questions that you wouldn't think to ask.

Mrs. Everett had just finished her lunch when the bell rang. "Oh, goodness, where does the time go? You're welcome to stay a few minutes longer, and I'll write you a late pass. Or you can come back before or after school—whichever works best for you. What's important is that you know I'm here if you ever need someone to talk to," Mrs. Everett said, looking at LaTrell.

"I think I'd better go to class. We're presenting projects in English," LaTrell said.

"No problem. Remember, I'm here if you need me," Mrs. Everett said.

"Thanks! I won't forget, "LaTrell said, looking back and smiling while she waved.

December 5

Mama, I finally did it!!! I listened and followed your directions (smile). I told Dad about the cyber-bully. I also got a chance to talk to Mrs. Everett, the school counselor, and I feel so much better.

Guess who was behind this? Kevin! Do you remember him? He's always been in my classes since elementary school. You even bought him a souvenir during a third-grade field trip. Do you remember now? I bet you're just as shocked as I am. Kevin's always been friendly. I wonder why he turned on me. You know what, Mama? I've discovered so much about myself. Even though what Kevin did was wrong, I forgive him. I know I get this from you, because I wanted to fight whoever it was so bad, but now I don't. I pray when Kevin meets with Mrs. Everett she can help him deal with any hurt or problems he's having. I don't want to ever go through anything like this again. I'm not going to keep a big secret. I can't handle all that pressure. I need to apologize to Dad and Daryl. I haven't been very nice lately. Mama, you can smile again. I promise I've learned my lesson. I miss you so much. Love you!

Chapter 5 Questions

1. Have you ever kept a secret for so long that when you finally told it, you felt like a weight lifted off your shoulders?

2. In this chapter, LaTrell tried to handle a serious situation by herself. Have you ever taken a matter into your own hands? What was the outcome? What would you have done if you had been in LaTrell's shoes?

3. The power of forgiveness is like a superpower. Forgiveness can help restore the person who forgives to emotional wholeness and physical well-being. However, failing to forgive only holds us down. Is there someone you have been mad at for some time now and would like to forgive? A teacher? A friend? A family member?

<u>Six</u>

Blindsided!

One Monday morning while LaTrell made her bed, she overheard Daryl talking to Luis.

"Hey, Dad, you know what we haven't done in a long time?" Daryl asked.

"What's that, son?" Luis said.

"We haven't gone to the movies," Daryl said.

"Yeah! You're right. I don't think we've been since your mom died," Luis said.

"Yeah, I don't think so either. A lot of my classmates have been talking about the movie *Alexander and the Terrible, Horrible, No Good, Very Bad Day*. Since it's an older movie, it's the $2 feature for the month of February. Do you think we can go see it?" Daryl asked.

"How about we go on Valentine's Day, after I get off from work? We haven't had any kind of family outing since your birthday," Luis said.

"Oh yeah, oh yeah!" Daryl said. "It'll be just like old times."

A slight smile came across LaTrell's face as she positioned the last pillow. She also missed the family outings they had all taken when Paulina was living. Paulina had believed in keeping the family culturally exposed, and so they had gone to plays, movies, gospel concerts, and a variety of restaurants.

February 5

Morning, Mama! It's a new year, and we're already in February. Guess what? This morning, me and Kevin meet with Mrs. Everett. Oops! I meant Kevin and I (I could hear you correct me :)). I can't wait to tell you how that goes. I gotta hurry up and eat my breakfast. Love you!

LaTrell's school had been back from Christmas break only a little over a month, but she was already ready for another vacation. Principal Willingham required LaTrell and Kevin to attend counseling sessions separately, but this Wednesday morning, they would be attending a session together, until the administration could work out Kevin's punishment. Although LaTrell wanted to understand why Kevin had taken part in cyber-bullying her, her nerves begin to stir up again.

LaTrell arrived at Mrs. Everett's office as usual at 8:00 a.m. Mrs. Everett paused from doing paperwork to greet her and motioned for LaTrell to take a seat at the round table. Once seated, LaTrell pulled a *Seventeen* magazine out of her book bag. As she flipped through the pages, the office door opened slowly; then a pair of eyes peered around the door.

"Good morning. Is it okay to come in?" a deep voice said.

LaTrell and Mrs. Everett both looked up at the same time to see Kevin waiting for a response.

"Yes, Kevin. Come on in," Mrs. Everett said, getting up from her desk.

Kevin sat across the table from LaTrell without making eye contact with her. Mrs. Everett sat in between them and placed a bowl of mints in the middle of the table, alongside a box of Kleenex.

"I'm glad you're both here this morning," Mrs. Everett said, looking at LaTrell and Kevin. "I know we met one-on-one the last few weeks before Christmas break; I hope those sessions gave you time to calm down. Now, I want to open the floor and give you two the opportunity to ask each other questions or state how you feel in a respectful way. However, you may speak only if you are holding this talking hand paddle," Mrs. Everett added, pointing to it as if it were a piece of jewelry.

"Who wants to go first?" she asked.

LaTrell looked at Kevin. Kevin looked back at LaTrell. LaTrell reached for the talking-hand paddle and asked, as tears formed in her eyes, "Kevin, why do you hate me? Have I ever made you mad? What did I do to make you want to cyber-bully me?"

"Kevin, this would be a good time to share what you told me in our one-on-one sessions," Mrs. Everett interjected.

Kevin looked up from the table and at LaTrell. His eyes still appeared as if they had no life. "We've been cool since the first grade, LaTrell. I remembered how nice Ms. Paulina was to me and everyone else. Before she died, I used to see your whole family out having a good time. I would daydream about what my life would be like if I lived in the same house with both of my parents." Kevin paused and looked at LaTrell.

LaTrell's eyes grew wide. This was the first she had ever heard anyone say they wished for a family like hers.

Kevin continued, "When your mom died, I was

so sad. I secretly viewed her as my play mom. I thought you would become angry and feel unwanted, like me, but instead you remained the same, like nothing bothered you. You, your dad, and your brother still seem like one happy family. I guess I became jealous and wanted you to hurt like I do. That's why I sent those cruel e-mails. My cousin typed those mean words, and I sent the messages from an e-mail address I use for virtual gaming sites," Kevin said, with a look of regret.

"Hunh?" LaTrell said. "You don't think we miss my mom? I think about her every single day. I bet my dad and my brother do, too. I don't know what you're talking about, but my family isn't happy all the time. We're just doing the best we can to learn how to adjust to life without her."

"Kevin, what did you mean when you said you thought LaTrell would become angry and feel unwanted like you do?" Mrs. Everett asked.

Kevin slouched a little in his seat. He didn't seem to be in any rush to answer the question. After what seemed like a few minutes, he finally spoke.

"I hate my living situation. I feel unwanted because my mother and older siblings work a lot, so they don't spend any time with me. I don't know where my dad is. My aunt and cousins live with us, so I never get any privacy. This makes me very angry at times," Kevin said, looking at Mrs. Everett, then at LaTrell. He continued, "I figured since your mom was gone, your dad would have to work more and you and Daryl would know what it felt like to feel lonely and unwanted."

The more LaTrell listened to Kevin, the more she felt sorry for him. In the whole time she had known him, she could count on one hand the number of times she had seen his mom.

"Do you still feel that way?" Mrs. Everett asked.

"Yeah, I do. I don't know what I can do to make it better. But I realize now that I should not have taken my hurt out on LaTrell," Kevin said, sitting up in his chair. "I'm sorry, LaTrell. I didn't mean for the e-mails to go back and forth for so long. And I don't want to get you that upset again," he said, looking at her sincerely.

Mrs. Everett's eyes shifted from Kevin to LaTrell. LaTrell sensed that they were both waiting to see if she accepted Kevin's apology or not. *Mama, guide me on what to say*, LaTrell thought. Then she leaned forward, biting her lip.

"I don't like what you did. That really hurt my feelings. I hope you and your mama can spend some time together soon. And I . . . I forgive you," she said, feeling relieved.

"What? You do? You don't hate me?"

LaTrell slowly shook her head left to right. "No, I don't hate you. My mama used to say 'hate' is a strong word. I never knew about the things you said earlier. Even though what you did wasn't right, I kinda understand why you did what you did. My mama also taught me and my brother that it's better to let go of the grudge you hold against someone and forgive them—not to be friends with them again, but to prevent your body from holding on to any stress."

"No one has ever told me they forgive me," said Kevin, still looking caught off-guard by LaTrell's response.

"Do you promise never to be mean to me again?" LaTrell asked, with a serious face.

"Oh yeah, I promise," Kevin said, nodding his head up and down vigorously.

"Then I choose to forgive you," LaTrell said, giving him a look of deep understanding.

Just then, the first bell sounded, signaling all students to get to class.

"Well, I think this meeting was very productive," Mrs. Everett said, as she clapped her hands together. "How do you both feel now that you've gotten a chance to express yourselves?"

"Better!" LaTrell and Kevin said at the same time.

"Wonderful!" Mrs. Everett said, smiling widely at them. "LaTrell and Kevin, my door is always open. Please don't be strangers," she added, as she stood up from her seat, smoothing out her dress.

"I won't," LaTrell said. As she passed Mrs. Everett, she gave her a hug before opening the door.

"Um, is it okay if I come back tomorrow?" Kevin asked.

"You sure can, Kevin!" Mrs. Everett said, patting him on the back.

Later on that day, during lunch, LaTrell sat with Chandler and Shajuan to discuss a little of what had happened during her counseling session with Kevin.

"For real?" Shajuan said, crunching on chips.

"Dang, that explains why he acts like a weirdo sometimes," Chandler said, nodding his head.

"Too bad he's going to get a ten-day suspension," Shajuan said.

"Wait, what?" LaTrell asked.

"Girl, you haven't heard? The word on the street is that Principal Willingham is going to suspend Kevin for ten days," Shajuan said, still smacking on her chips.

"Yep! I heard the same thing," Chandler chimed in.

"Oh no! I need to see Principal Willingham now!" LaTrell said. She gathered her things and rushed out of the cafeteria as Chandler and Shajuan looked at each other and shrugged their shoulders.

On the way to the office, LaTrell spotted Principal Willingham in the hallway, moving students along.

Hi, Principal Willingham. Can I speak with you for a second?" LaTrell asked, trying to catch her breath.

"Sure. Is everything okay?" he asked, taking her to the side by the elbow.

"I'm okay, but during lunch I heard a rumor that you plan to suspend Kevin for ten days. Is that true?" LaTrell asked, with a worried look.

"Boy, it doesn't take long for rumors to start around here, does it?" he said shaking his head. "No, it's not true. I haven't decided on Kevin's punishment yet, but there will be one. Why are you concerned?" Principal Willingham asked, with one eyebrow raised.

"Well, during the counseling session this morning, Kevin shared a lot of what he's going through at home and how he feels. It has a lot to do with the cyber-bullying. I think he should be punished, but not for ten days. Maybe part of his punishment can be to enroll in the Cross-age peer mentor program," LaTrell said, feeling as if she'd just come up with a bright idea. The Cross-age mentor program matched a high school student (mentor) with a middle school student (mentee) for the purpose of guiding and supporting the mentee in many areas of her academic, social, and emotional development.

"A mentor program, huh? Okay, I'll take your idea into consideration, LaTrell. Is there anything else?" Principal Willingham asked.

"That was it. Oh, I also told Kevin that I forgive him. My mama told me it's better to forgive and not hold on to negative stress. That cyber-bullying really stressed me out," LaTrell said.

"Really? LaTrell, I must say, you are wise beyond your years. I think we could all learn a lesson or two from your mother," he said with a chuckle. "Now, you better run along so you aren't late for class."

"Okay, bye!" LaTrell said, waving as she walked away.

***

For the next few days, LaTrell felt nervous. She knew Kevin would probably learn of his punishment at the end of the week, and she hoped Principal Willingham would go easy on him.

Besides, sitting at home wasn't going to help Kevin be a better person.

When Friday finally arrived, it was like any other normal day. Throughout the day, LaTrell looked to see if Kevin acted differently. When she didn't notice any change, she assumed he would receive his punishment on another day. When school let out, she was walking down the main hallway toward the school exit, when she saw Kevin and his mother coming out of the front office. LaTrell stopped in her tracks like a deer caught in headlights.

"Hey, LaTrell," Kevin said.

"Oh, LaTrell, I'm so sorry. Kevin knows better. I don't raise my kids to mistreat others," Kevin's mother said, as she placed her arm around LaTrell's shoulders to hug her.

"I already apologized to her mom," Kevin said, sounding aggravated.

"I forgive Kevin, Ms. Lyons. He promised that he wouldn't bully me or anyone else again," LaTrell said, looking at Kevin for confirmation.

"Well, he better not, or he's going to find himself placed in a juvenile detention center. He was spared a harsh punishment, and he has you to thank for it. He was given only a two-day suspension. Plus, he is required to participate in this Cross-age mentoring program for the rest of the school year," Ms. Lyons said, looking at a piece of paper she was holding and shaking her head in disappointment.

"Thanks for speaking up for me, LaTrell," Kevin muttered, with his head down.

"You're welcome," LaTrell said, looking from Ms. Lyons to Kevin.

"Come on. Let's go. I'm late for work," Ms. Lyons said, as she nudged Kevin to prompt him to start walking. "See you around, LaTrell. Tell your dad and Daryl hello."

"I will," LaTrell said softly.

She quietly followed behind them and listened to Ms. Lyons fussing at Kevin some more. *Kevin can't seem to catch a break*, she thought.

As soon as LaTrell got home, she hurriedly changed into a tank top and a pair of shorts and positioned herself on the bed to prepare for her routine nap. Before dozing off, she retrieved her journal from the top drawer.

February 7
Hey Mama! I'm back. See, I told you I was going to do better. I know you can't wait to hear about the counseling session I had on Wednesday. I didn't know what to expect,

but it went well. I told Kevin that I forgive him. Mama, I feel so sorry for Kevin. He says he's lonely and feels unwanted. No one spends time with him. His mother works too much. And you know what he said? That he secretly looked at you as his play mom!!! I never knew that, but it's not hard to believe. A lot of the kids in the neighborhood admired you. Kevin learned his punishment today. He got suspended for two days and is required to participate in the Cross-age mentoring program. I hope he learned his lesson and never bullies anyone else. Ooh, Mama! I just did a huge yawn. I'm so tired. I'm gonna take a nap now. Love you!

***

LaTrell could always tell when Valentine's Day was near: the teachers were less moody, and the students acted nicer than usual. The attitude change was in hopes of receiving a special Valentine's Day card or expensive candy. This year, Valentine's Day was on a Friday. Students arrived at school wearing various shades of red and pink. Balloons and streamers decorated the hallways. LaTrell and Shajuan were standing in front of their lockers, talking before school, as usual, when out of the corner of LaTrell's eye she saw Chandler approaching them. He had both of his hands behind his back.

Shajuan stopped talking when Chandler got closer. "Why are you walking with both of your hands behind your back?" she asked.

"Because I can mouth from the South," Chandler said, rolling his eyes toward the ceiling.

"Boy, what are you hiding?" Shajuan asked, attempting to look behind Chandler. LaTrell tried to get a peek, too.

Chandler took two steps back, shaking his head. "You two are the nosiest girls I know. Even nosier than my grandma." Then he added, "LaTrell, you've gone through a lot these last few months, so I thought I would get you a lil' some'n-some'n to lift your spirits." He pulled a white card from behind his back and handed it over to LaTrell.

LaTrell's and Shajuan's mouths dropped.

"Um, *hello*! What about me?" Shajuan asked, placing her right hand on her hip.

Chandler ignored Shajuan and kept his eyes on LaTrell.

LaTrell had never gotten anything from Chandler. She took the card from him and looked at it. The front of the card said "Special Valentine" in red.

"Girl, don't just stare at it. Open it!" Shajuan said anxiously.

LaTrell glanced at Chandler and then ripped open the card. A $5 gift card for a Dairy Queen Blizzard was taped on the right side.

The left side read, in Chandler's handwriting:

LaTrell,
Believe it or not, somehow you manage to
make me smile every day.
So to you, a special friend of mine,
Happy Valentine's Day!
Your Boy, Chandler (Chan the Man)

"Aw, thank you, Chandler," LaTrell said, blushing. "This is so sweet."

"I'm glad you like it. It's the least I could do," Chandler said.

"Well, what do *I* need to go through to get a card?" Shajuan asked.

She was about to ask another question but stopped when she noticed the way LaTrell and Chandler stood there, looking at each other.

When the second warning bell sounded, Shajuan grabbed LaTrell by the elbow and said, "We better get to class before we get detention."

"I'll see y'all at lunch," Chandler said.

"Bye, Chan the Man! Thanks again," LaTrell said, smiling.

All three walked away, feeling differently. LaTrell felt special. Chandler poked his chest out as if he had just scored a touchdown. Shajuan couldn't put her finger on the look exchange she had witnessed between LaTrell and Chandler, but she knew something was up.

***

"LaTrell, hurry up in there! We have to get a good seat at the movies," Daryl said, as he knocked on the bathroom door. The Wigginses were finally on their way to the movies. Daryl had been talking nonstop about the book *Alexander and the Terrible, Horrible, No Good, Very Bad Day*. He hoped the movie was just as funny and exciting.

Daryl talked so much that he didn't notice that Luis turned the volume up a notch on the radio to hear his favorite song in the car. LaTrell rolled her eyes to the sky as she smacked on her bubble gum and blew big bubbles. Before long, they had arrived at the movie theater.

"I think this parking space will work," Luis said, putting the gear shift in park.

As soon as the car came to a halt, so did Daryl's talking.

"Listen, before we go inside, I want you to know that I'm only buying one jumbo popcorn for all three of us to share, and three bottles of water. Nothing else! That means no candy!" Luis said, looking at LaTrell and Daryl with a straight face. "We'll get something to eat after the movies. Do you understand?" he added, with one eyebrow raised.

"Yes," LaTrell and Daryl said.

It didn't matter where they went—Luis always made a point of reviewing what he expected from them and what he would and would not pay for.

Daryl swung the door open and hopped out of the car. He hadn't been this happy since his birthday party.

When they reached the box office, Luis said, "One adult and two child tickets for *Alexander and the Terrible, Horrible, No Good, Very Bad Day*, please."

"That will be twenty-one dollars," the cashier said.

Luis handed her the money, and Daryl reached for the movie tickets.

Once they were inside, Daryl handed the tickets to the ticket collector. "Here you go!" he said.

"Thank you! Theater number three is to your right. Enjoy your movie," the ticket collector said.

"We will!" Daryl said, hurrying to the concessions counter.

"Slow down, son!" Luis said trying to keep up with Daryl.

While they were standing in line, a woman carrying food approached LaTrell. "Well, long time no see!" she said.

LaTrell turned to see that it was Ms. Alice from the undergarments store. Her hair was in large, long candy curls, and there were no eyeglasses sitting on top of her head this time. Instead, Ms. Alice's lips were neatly painted with a dark red lipstick that complemented the cream shirt and skinny jeans she wore with brown boots.

"Oh, hi, Ms. Alice!" LaTrell said, giving her a side hug.

"Ms. Alice! I almost didn't recognize you," Luis said, smiling.

"Who is that?" Daryl whispered in LaTrell's ear.

"That's Ms. Alice. She works at this store that sells all sorts of bras and underwear. She helped me choose the right bra size," LaTrell said, with a grin.

"Eww," Daryl said, moving away from LaTrell.

"What movie are you here to see?" Luis asked.

"I'm here with my nephew, Chase, to see *Alexander and the Terrible, Horrible, No Good, Very Bad Day*," Ms. Alice said. "He's over there, playing the arcade games," she added, pointing.

"So are we!" Luis said.

"Well, maybe we can all sit together," Ms. Alice said, sounding excited.

Sit together? This is our family time, LaTrell said to herself.

Daryl whispered again, "Why is Dad smiling so hard?"

LaTrell looked at Luis and then at Ms. Alice. Both of their faces were frozen in smiles. LaTrell immediately felt some kind of way. Luis hadn't smiled this much in a long time. *What is it about Ms. Alice that's making him smile so much?* LaTrell wondered.

"Oh, Dad, it's our turn!" Daryl said.

Daryl's outburst interrupted the awkward moment between Luis and Ms. Alice, and they snapped back to reality.

"Okay, I'm going to grab my nephew and head in. I'll save seats for you guys!" Ms. Alice said, waving and walking away.

LaTrell watched Ms. Alice until she was out of

sight. She turned her head to the right and saw Kevin standing with a teenage boy placing an order. LaTrell made her way over to them.

"Hey, Kevin!" LaTrell said, tapping him on the shoulder.

"Hey, LaTrell!" Kevin said when he turned around.

"Is this your big brother?" LaTrell asked.

Kevin and the older boy chuckled. "No, this is Rick, my mentor from the Cross-age program. Today is our social outing," he said, smiling.

"Oh, hi, I'm LaTrell. I'm one of Kevin's classmates," LaTrell said, waving. "What movie are you going to see?"

"Nice to meet you," Rick said, extending his hand to LaTrell. "We're going to see *Alexander and the Terrible, Horrible, No Good, Very Bad Day*."

"We are, too. I hope it's just as funny as the previews," LaTrell said.

"Come on, LaTrell!" Daryl yelled.

"I have to go. I'll see you later, Kevin," LaTrell said.

After getting their popcorn and drinks, the Wigginses walked to the third theater door. When they came around the corner, Luis spotted Ms. Alice standing up, waving both hands. Luis raised up the big bucket of popcorn he held to acknowledge her. Luis led the way up the stairs and to the row where Ms. Alice was. Luis sat in between LaTrell and Daryl. Next to Daryl was Chase, then Ms. Alice. Not long after they sat, the lights dimmed and upcoming-movie trailers came on one after the other.

"We got here just in time," Daryl said, grabbing a handful of popcorn.

At last the movie began. The main character, Alexander, woke up to find that everything was going terribly wrong. He didn't go through it alone, though; his family experienced bad days, too. After each negative occurrence, Alexander experienced a range of emotions. One minute, he was in a bad mood. Next, that mood turned into jealousy, then on to frustration and in some instances rage. Somehow, he managed to deal with each of these emotions.

While the movie played, LaTrell found herself relating to how Alexander felt. She had experienced all of those emotions when Paulina died and had dealt with some again because of the cyber-bullying situation.

Despite the misfortunes that happened to Alexander and his family, there were a lot of funny scenes in the movie. No one was more tickled than

Daryl and Chase. They bent over and held their stomachs from laughing so hard.

I wish I felt like laughing, LaTrell said to herself.

Through it all, Alexander's family pulled together to work as a team. The movie concluded with the disasters working in everyone's favor.

"That was awesome!" Daryl said, pumping his fist up and down as if he were tooting a train's horn.

"I'm glad you enjoyed it," Luis said.

"Dad, can we come to the movies on the Fridays you get paid?" Daryl asked.

Luis's eyes grew big. "I don't know about that, son. We'll see how it goes." Then he said, "Ms. Alice, how did you like the movie?"

"I thought it was cute. Chase really had a ball," Ms. Alice said, patting her nephew's shoulders.

"Hey, we're going to grab a bite to eat. Would you all like to join us?" Luis asked.

LaTrell looked up at Luis, feeling offended. *What is he doing?* she wondered.

"Chase, are you ready to go home, or would you like to get something to eat with the Wiggins family?" Ms. Alice asked.

"I want to get something to eat. I'm starving," Chase said.

Well, that's just great. I guess I won't be telling Dad about my situation tonight, LaTrell said to herself.

They walked out of the theater and to their cars.

LaTrell looked at Daryl, and he seemed just fine with having Ms. Alice and Chase come along to dinner. The fact was, Daryl was happy that he had someone around his age whom he could interact with.

"Okay, meet us at the Red Robin Burger place on Pines Boulevard," Luis said.

"Got it! See you in a few," Ms. Alice replied, giving him her usual smile.

Before Luis closed his car door and put on his seat belt, LaTrell went all in with the questions.

"Dad, why didn't you ask me and Daryl first if we wanted other people to join us for dinner?" She continued, "And why did we have to sit next to Ms. Alice and her nephew in the movies? It's just supposed to be us."

When LaTrell asked the second question, Luis was in the middle of adjusting his mirrors. He paused and looked over at LaTrell.

"LaTrell, you sound upset. I'm sorry I didn't ask you and your brother about inviting them. I honestly didn't think you all would mind. And do I detect a little jealousy?" asked Luis. "There's nothing wrong with sharing our time with others. What's *really* bothering you?"

LaTrell sat back in the front seat and shrugged her shoulders. "Nothing, I guess," she said.

The drive to Red Robin was less than five minutes away. Once inside, they were greeted by a hostess, who then led them to a huge booth with an oversize table.

Daryl and Chase sat on opposite sides of the table and slid in closest to the wall. LaTrell scooted in after Daryl. Luis and Ms. Alice sat at the ends of the table. Daryl and Chase immediately picked up where they had left off at the movies. Chase was the same age and height as Daryl, but slimmer. He had a head full of curly hair and wore a pair of frameless eyeglasses.

LaTrell leaned on the table with her right elbow and cupped her chin with her right hand. Luis and Ms. Alice discussed how the cost of movie tickets had increased over the past year.

I hope they come take our order soon. Everyone has somebody to talk to besides me, LaTrell thought. She then began reflecting on the Valentine's Day card she had received from Chandler earlier that day.

"LaTrell, you seem to be in deep thought over there. Are you okay?" Ms. Alice asked.

Daryl stopped talking and looked over at LaTrell.

"Yes, I'm just hungry," LaTrell said, snapping out of her daze.

"Are you sure? Wow! I can't get over how mature you look now," Ms. Alice said, with a smile.

The waitress saved LaTrell from responding when she came to the table and took everyone's order.

"So, what are your plans for Easter?" Ms. Alice asked.

LaTrell looked at Luis out of the corner of her eye.

"I'm not sure. I think we may have dinner at our house, or maybe go over to my sister's house," Luis said.

"If you would like to, you all are welcome to come to my house," Ms. Alice said.

LaTrell and Daryl looked at each other.

"Thank you for the invite. I will keep that in mind," Luis said smiling.

"There goes that wide jack-o'-lantern smile again," Daryl said, nudging LaTrell.

Chase was too busy cleaning his glasses to pay attention to LaTrell and Daryl. Before Ms. Alice could say another word, the waitress arrived with the food. Daryl and Chase became energized all over again and licked their lips. LaTrell was starving, too. Luis and Alice helped pass the food to the right people and made sure everyone had what they needed. For a few minutes, the only noises were slurping, smacking, and satisfied food sounds.

Finally, Luis spoke. "So, how often do you have Chase?" he asked.

"Two weekends out of the month," Chase blurted out.

"My brother, William, Chase's father, has to work a few weekends each month. And his mother, Lisa, is a traveling nurse. I coordinate my weekends off with the days my brother has to go in," Ms. Alice said.

"Well, aren't you a nice auntie," Luis said, chuckling.

"The best!" Chase called out.

Everyone at the table laughed, except LaTrell, who stuffed her mouth with food to prevent herself from doing so.

"Can you bring Chase over to the house on the weekends that you have him?" Daryl asked Ms. Alice.

LaTrell stopped chewing and gave Daryl a crazy look.

"That's up to your dad, Daryl," Ms. Alice said.

All eyes shifted to Luis.

"Sure, I don't have a problem with it," Luis said.

"Yes!" Daryl and Chase said, giving each other a high five.

LaTrell wiped her mouth and pushed her plate away. She suddenly wasn't hungry anymore. Daryl and Chase slurped the last bit of their milk shakes; then Luis and Ms. Alice stacked the trays and plates at the edge of the table for the waitress to collect.

"Do you guys want dessert, or are you too full?" Ms. Alice asked.

Luis cut his eyes at Daryl, as if daring him to say yes.

"No, thanks, I'm good," Daryl said in a hesitant voice.

"I'm stuffed," LaTrell said.

"I don't have any room left, Auntie," Chase said, patting his stomach.

"Then that means it's time to go," Luis said.

Luis handed the waitress the bill payment and told her to keep the change. Everyone eased out of the booth to stand up.

"Dad, I need to use the bathroom," Daryl said.

"Me too!" Chase said.

"Go ahead. We'll wait for you right here," Luis said.

LaTrell sat on a bench in the lobby and continue to watch Luis and Ms. Alice.

"Is there a number where I can reach you to arrange an outing with the boys?" Ms. Alice asked, while holding her mobile phone.

Wait a minute! A number? LaTrell said to herself.

"Oh yeah, that's right—I almost forgot," Luis said.

After Luis gave her his number, Ms. Alice said, "Okay, I have you programmed in my phone now. I sure hope Mr. Chase doesn't have you rethinking your answer."

"Nope, my answer still stands. Besides, he and Daryl seem to be the right kind of company for each other," Luis said, giving her that same wide smile.

"I agree," Ms. Alice said.

Daryl and Chase walked up to Luis and Ms. Alice. Daryl noticed both of them sharing a big smile again, and he turned and looked at LaTrell. She looked back at him as if her eyes could shoot darts. Then Daryl turned his attention back to Luis and Ms. Alice.

"Okay, let's head out," Luis said, jingling his keys.

They all said their goodbyes in the parking lot. On the way home, Daryl leaned up in between the driver's and passenger seats to talk, like he always did.

"Dad, I had fun tonight. Thank you for the movies and dinner," Daryl said.

"You're welcome," Luis said.

"Hey, Dad, why were you smiling so much tonight?" Daryl asked.

"Smiling? Who, me?" Luis asked.

"Yes," LaTrell chimed in. "You haven't smiled that much since . . . Mama was alive," she said, as her voice trailed off.

"Oh boy! I wasn't aware that I smiled that much this evening. You two really watch your dad, hunh?" Luis asked.

"Uh-hunh!" LaTrell and Daryl replied, looking at Luis.

Luis opened his mouth, about to say something, but decided not to. All of a sudden, he felt ashamed and guilty. *Was I smiling that much? Is it too soon to enjoy myself with another adult woman?* he asked himself. They drove the rest of the way home in silence.

February 15

Hey Mama! We had a long day yesterday. I went straight to sleep after the movies. First, let me tell you about your boy Chandler. He got me a Valentine's Day card. This was my first time ever getting a card from him. But not just any card— a "special" card. My stomach felt like it had butterflies flapping around inside. What does that mean? Oh, and the movie was very good, but being there wasn't the same without you. We are still trying to get used to being a family of three. :(Do you remember Ms. Alice, who fitted me for my bra? She and her nephew attended the same movie and sat with us. Dad was acting very strange. He talked and smiled more than normal. What do you think that means? Mama, do you all watch movies in heaven? Are parties allowed? I've been wondering what you do all day. I miss you so much. Love you!

Chapter 6 Questions

1. Have you ever had a relationship change when you've lost touch with someone you were once close to? Or have you developed a relationship with someone you never thought you would bond with?

2. Hiding behind a mask is a way of disappearing—being invisible. When you wear a mask for a long time, you don't really know yourself or what you're feeling. Being true to yourself allows you to become emotionally free. What truths would you like to reveal?

About the Author

Dr. Chenee' Gilbert has been an educator for twenty years. Her vision is to help the youth of ages (5-17) communicate their feelings and reprogram their mindsets to achieve their fullest potential. Dr. Gilbert's latest book "Blindsided" the second book of Dr. Gilbert's three-part Dear Grief series is now available.

www.ingramcontent.com/pod-product-compliance
Lightning Source LLC
Chambersburg PA
CBHW071917290426
44110CB00013B/1385